Homosexuality

...."The Untold Story"

Luby Martin

authorHOUSE®

AuthorHouse™
1663 Liberty Drive
Bloomington, IN 47403
www.authorhouse.com
Phone: 1 (800) 839-8640

Published by AuthorHouse   11/19/2016

ISBN: 978-1-5246-5027-8 (sc)
ISBN: 978-1-5246-5026-1 (e)

Print information available on the last page.

Any people depicted in stock imagery provided by Thinkstock are models,
and such images are being used for illustrative purposes only.
Certain stock imagery © Thinkstock.

This book is printed on acid-free paper.

Because of the dynamic nature of the Internet, any web addresses or links contained in
this book may have changed since publication and may no longer be valid. The views
expressed in this work are solely those of the author and do not necessarily reflect the
views of the publisher, and the publisher hereby disclaims any responsibility for them.

KJV
Scripture quotations marked KJV are from the Holy Bible, King James Version
(Authorized Version). First published in 1611. Quoted from the KJV Classic
Reference Bible, Copyright © 1983 by The Zondervan Corporation.

Genesis 1:26 And *God* said let us make *man* in our own *image,* after our *likeness...*
Genesis 1:27 So created man in his own image in the *image of God* created him; *male and female created* he them.
Genesis 1:28 And God blessed them, and God said unto them, Be fruitful, and multiply, and replenish the earth, and subdue it: and have dominion over the fish of the sea, fowl of the air and all creature upon the earth.

Contents

Preface

In those opening, three short verses (a tenth of a page), God... the creator of all, lays out mankind's basic eternal plan upon earth. And DOMA (Defense of Marriage Act) of our American Constitution support those three short verses. But five Supreme Court Judges, in a document; requiring more than seventy pages, thought it necessary to inform God, he needed an amendment to his creation of man and woman.

In the above three Bible verses, God explains to man, he used "himself" as the pattern to create him. This meant, giving man God like powers, like himself, to have dominion over all the earth. In other words, making man a co-creator with God.

Later, God explains to man, he divided him into two parts male and female for a specific purpose. Like man, all earthly animals and other species are made compatible (male and female) to continue their indefinite existent on earth. This will be done through the process, the English Language describe as... Procreation.

And now, in the world of today, all creatures has continued their cycle of procreation from the beginning; as God Commanded. But man...the co-creator with God; has become confused about his natural mating partner for the continuity of his specie. And worse than that, he has no shame about this confusion. Why man has become confuse is the question this book will answer. The question...that the so call experts has failed to answer down through the ages. The main way this will be done, is by revealing the first act of Homosexuality.

But more importantly, this book will prove, that by enforcing a five-four Supreme Court Ruling, declaring DOMA unconstitutional; goes against people Religious teaching: and, a direct violation of their First Amendment Right. Not only does their Religion warn them "not" to support Same Sex Marriage; it teaches them *Acts 5:29:"We ought to obey God rather than men".* Just for clarity, "men" is referring to the Govern*men*t.

This book will make it clear, that Homosexuality is a choice. This choice goes back to man's first choice made in the Garden of Eden by Adam and Eve between good and evil.

It will be explained, that the choice of Homosexuality is also a personal matter. Because of its ungodly nature, and against most Religious teaching(Bible) in America, it should be kept in privacy. This should be done with the familiar axiom..."that what you do in privacy of your home, is your own business". And...because of its sexual nature, it is not the business of the public, "who you do and what you do" in the privacy of your Bedroom.

This book is not trying to stop ones choice of Homosexuality, because choice is part of God's divine plan. With that, we hope to clear up the fact, that Heterosexuals are not judging Homosexuals when quoting scriptures.

Although "Trends" change from generation to generation; the word of God never change. Meaning that, scripture interpretations on issues like Homosexuality are very clear; to the point, and consistent throughout time.

This book makes it clear, that by Homosexuality violating nature ...it affects nature around us in the atmosphere. Why Homosexuality is an issue that the media should be careful in pushing on a world, that the future of it...exist...only through procreation.

This book will point out, that "legalizing Same Sex Marriage" in this nation was handle improperly. Until it is handle the right way, it will be an ongoing controversy.

Drawing from the sacred words of the Bible and American History; this book explains the "only" fair solution to both sides of this issue. This was not an issue that was suppose to be the decision of nine people(Supreme Court Judges) to start with; regardless of their intellect and position. Nevertheless, we only hope, that after reading this "fair" solution on this controversial issue; that the powers to be will take a differ approach on this matter.

Throughout this book, it explains...when the Gay community... the media...the Supreme Court, "Forces" this nation to indulge the publicity of "your" Homosexuality; it puts us all in grave danger. This book will reveal, how Homosexuality, is the second worse sin-crime on earth: with murder being first.

This book is the voice of those who honor the Bible teaching on Homosexuality, and... those that does not support the publicity of this behavior in our nation.

This book is to inform us, that Homosexuality is "unlike" any other issue we have dealt with...in America. Also, this book explains, why it is important as a nation, that we get this issue under control. Same Sex relationships strikes at the very essence of the future of mankind. This book will show with Bible History and American's facts; the consistency of God's word, on other issues similar to this. This book will connect all the dots, that has led to publicizing mass Homosexuality in America of today.

We will prove, based on the famous horrific destruction of Sodom and Gomorrah, those who indulge or support this behavior are "Most Expendable" in the eyes of God.

Despite the "redundancy" and "anti-gay" stand, I have taken in this book to emphasize certain points; some...that remain Gay all their life, will be given a fair end by Jesus Christ. That's why I challenge you(LGBT) to read the entire book...a surprising end.

Introduction

To qualify me as an expert on this topic, was an event that happen in my life about forty years ago. I underwent a unique religious experience, that left me with a Gift of interpretation that help me explain things that baffle today's Historians and experts. I also discovered, that I can come up with a plausible explanation, to many questions that has been ask down through the years, on various unexplained topics. As a reference to that claim; read *"The Half Have Never Been Told"* by *Jolomark Retunah;* with a focus on the chapter, *"Did you Know"*?

While writing that particular book, I discovered that, if one approach any topic whether fiction or true, with the attitude of exploration and discovery, one will always arrived at the truth. The above mention book has many examples of that as well.

My biggest concern after being inspired to write this book, was: What tone should I take in writing it? After thinking on that, I begin to be hit with many questions and thoughts on the Homosexual issue. Here are some of those questions and thoughts.

What does the Bible say about this behavior? Is Same Sex Relationships the Liberty and Freedom our founding Fathers were referring too? Are both the Old Testament(OT) Law and the New Testament(NT) scriptures consistent on this issue? When the NT say, Jesus was tempted in all points as we: did that include Homosexuality? Why was there such negative consequences in the Bible for people that practice this lifestyle? Are their any scriptures that favor Same Sex Marriage in the OT and NT of the Bible. Is endorsing this behavior through the media sending the right message to our Children? Is it right for Same Sex Couples to raise children? Was there gender bias with the three Female Supreme Court Judges in their vote declaring DOMA unconstitutional? Is publicizing Same Sex Relationships in America, sending the right message to the rest of the World? Although I plan to answer all these questions in this book; by pondering over this; I received this revelation:

This book is to act as a message. My job is to use Bible History and American facts to demonstrate the consistency of God's word. I am not to be happy when proving God's word with examples of horrific destruction for the practice of Homosexuality. Neither am I to get upset like the prophet Jonah when things doesn't happen as predicted. I am to write any pertinent information that is reveal to me on this issue: whether I like it or not. I must allow my spirit to flow freely on this issue. That is the only way to arrive at the truth. Because, that is the duty of a true witness of the Gospel of Jesus Christ.

Unknowingly, over the years, God has given me many life lessons on this subject matter; of which I plan to share in this book. These lessons are to help us understand the tragedy in supporting and publicizing Same Sex relationships. Because, the doers and supporters of this behavior, doesn't understand; that violating God's word whether a believer or not... has consequences. Also, by not giving the Homosexual a thorough understanding that their condition is a "curse"...born out of the darkest of evil; they will not seek to correct it.

To start this message off; I like to present this thought. Isn't it strange, how there are no movies or T.V. Programs that shares stories of how someone overcame the Homosexual curse? The main reason for that...people doesn't realize this behavior is a curse.

From my experience, when one is made aware that they are cursed, the normal reaction is; how to break it or get from under it? That is what I hope that this book can do.

We hope to make the public aware that Homosexuality is a curse. People doesn't normally parade a curse like its a "badge of honor". Especially, if it is described in the Bible as an *"Abomination"*. Many that find themselves in this predicament usually keep it to themselves: they are the smart ones. Some curses only affect the person with it. But the "PUBLICITY" of the Homosexual curse in this nation, affects the whole nation as I will prove.

Same Sex Relationship is the most controversial and talked about topic in our Nation and the world. Why is it such a talked about topic? You can get many differ answers to that question. However, my immediate response to that question is; first of all, this was not a decision of the Supreme Court to legalize Same Sex Marriage in our nation. This behavior affects the very foundation of Human existent. The Supreme court's five-four ruling, questions...God's plan on the continuity of the human Species. The decision to publicize and promote this behavior in our country affects every American.

One thing that I like to clear up, and that is, there is nothing wrong for a man NOT to desire the sexual pleasure of a woman. And equally, there is nothing wrong for a woman NOT to desire the sexual pleasure of a man. But there is something inherently wrong with a man wanting another man in a sexual way as he would a woman. And a woman the same with another woman as she would a man. The Bible makes this clear.

People does not realize, that being single and not desiring the opposite sex, can suggest that you are a complete person and doesn't need to find another half. Also, your life may have been predestine to be a servant for God with singularity of purpose. Your life as a single person could be chosen to keep a balance in the world.

If you cannot recognize that desiring sexually a member of the same gender is out of sync with nature...then...what does that say about you in relation to animals? Animals, instinctively know their correct mating partner for the continuity of their species. For all those who think, that the Homosexual behavior is alright, I hope that this book can help modify your thinking as well.

What I hope to accomplish in this book, is a never heard of explanation of what constitute the Same Sex Relationship behavior.

Many things must be accepted before we can come to an adequate conclusion of how to handle the Homosexual issue. All the information in my research seems to come from a bias approach. I am not trying to be bias on the Same Sex issue; but informative. Also, I hope to give a good explanation of why ancient Bible truths were left for our society of today on this issue.

What really surprised me, in my preliminary research on this subject, is that, there are no experts in this field. When I say no experts, I am not referring to the Bible Historian that understand both OT law and NT scriptures on this subject. I am referring to no secular experts like Sociologist and Psychologist who suppose to be experts on human behavior.

One reason that there are no experts on this issue, is because, they decided to leave the Bible out of their understanding of this behavior. But during my research, when experts did reference the Bible(in support of this behavior) the scriptures were greatly misinterpreted. Alone this same train of thought; I discovered, that because Gay leaders could not adequately twist Bible scriptures to support their agenda, they came up with their own Bible. They call it "The Queen James Version" to offset the King James Version of the Bible; pertaining to this issue.

The King James Bible was the Gay leaders target for two reason. First, it is the most commonly used Bible in American's

Religions today. Secondly, because the King James Bible is very adamant and clear to the Church in not tolerating this behavior... this is referring to both OT Law and NT Scripture.

The Bible is the only Book that has both OT Laws and NT Scriptures on how to handle this behavior, and the danger it poses to ones Spiritual life. Experts of today, feel that OT Law and NT scriptures are too rigid on this behavior. What I hope to do, is explain why the Bible is so adamant about this issue.

I hope to give a clearer understanding of "Why" the Horrific destruction of Sodom and Gomorrah was left for our learning. And what the "Salt Statue" of Lot's wife during Sodom and Gomorrah destruction mean for people of today. Bible experts and Ministers of today, doesn't make it clear as to what the Salt statue of Lot's wife mean.

The destruction of Sodom and Gomorrah will be mention a great deal in this book. That's because, there is so much to be learn from the whole event of the destruction of Sodom and Gomorrah.

First, we need to understand...how can "everybody" in those two cities be "turned" to indulge in Same Sex Relationship, except for "four" people? Secondly, why God left on record such a horrific destruction for those who practice Same Sex relations.

The big problem in our nation is not Homosexuality, its the "publicity" of it. But even worst than that; our leaders, starting with the President, has misinterpreted the role they suppose to play. When American's leaders, misinterpret there role on a World wide controversial issue like this; it could have catastrophic consequences all over planet earth. The World look to America for leadership; with the thinking....if America's says its alright, then it should be okay. Even Hollywood, the entertaining industry of the nation, has misinterpreted their role in this matter as well.

I feel for forty years, God has given me the correct life lessons to write this book with interpretation skills. The interpretation skills that I possess are not interpreting from one language to another. My interpretation skills involves interpreting the message within the message. This is done by taking the composition of words in the English Language to a whole New level. This will be made clearer as this message unfold. The reference book mention above will make this method of interpretation "crystal" clear.

So far, all the material I have read and study in support of Homosexuality has seem to exclude the God factor. None of all the information I have research has yet to discuss with any kind of intelligent what is the cause of this behavior. At one time, the interest was...how to stop this ungodly and unnatural behavior. But now, it seems that the researchers, journalist and media are all about the acceptance of this life stye. This is because, people does not realize how the unnatural actions of this behavior, affect the very atmosphere: bringing about consequences of Biblical proportion.

The word "Cultural" was tossed around a great deal in my research. As to say, what was once a "hush" "hush" about this behavior; is no more.

In writing this book, I hope to answer a pressing question of my own. And that is: Why didn't Jesus deal with this issue when he was on earth? And a more modern day Question is: Why the Constitution of the United States did not leave a clarity in law (like the OT)on this behavior?

It has been said, all the Signers of the Declaration of Independence and the Constitution of the U.S. were readers of the Bible. I am sure at some point, they ran across this topic in the Bible. In fact, it has been said, many of our laws were based on Bible scriptures and religious Laws.

Let's take the first Ten Amendments of the America Constitution for an example. Whether by design or Godly intervention, our first Ten Amendments to the Constitution are actually, an analogue to the First Ten Commandments in the OT of the Bible.

What the first Ten Amendments to our Constitution represent, is that, we are God's Chosen People of today's World. Our Ten Amendments are like God's first favorite people...the Children of Israel; Ten Commandments introduced by Moses.

It is my belief, that this nation was design to represent a modern day Jerusalem. Which was Biblical described, as the Religious Headquarters of the world in the Old Testament. I have gone as far as to prove, that John's Revelation in the NT of the *"New Jerusalem coming down from Heaven"* was referring to America as its model. The above mention reference book can validate this as well.

I hope, that people who read this book know; regardless of how anti-gay I may come across; I am only trying to help. There are many ways you can view this book. My purpose is to try to give a clearer understanding of what Homosexuality really is.

It is written *(Prov. 4:7); Wisdom is the principal thing; therefore get wisdom; and with all thy getting get understanding.* Understanding is what is lacking in America on the Homosexual issue; from the President down to our grade school children.

Many people are trying to be acceptance and tolerant of this behavior...they feel there are no consequences for this life choice anymore.

When the Gospel was preached on this behavior, with emphasis on the death penalty, it kept people from making this behavior public. I am NOT talking about a death punishment in today's society; we are talking about Ministers Preaching what "USED" to be done in OT Law to those who practice Same Sex relationship. The adamant preaching of the Gospel alone, made a lot of people seek help for Homosexuality.

I hope that what is written in this book, will help those that are truly honest with themselves, recognize, that they doesn't want to be out of sync with nature. With that, know that they can get on natures track of their birth anatomy. Only one power as you will discover in this book has the ability to correct this malfunction in nature, and that is, "The Word of God"... the Bible.

Early Experience and Inspiration for this Book

The inspiration for this book is motivated by many things. After researching and found what the Bible had to say about Homosexuality...with the fact; that my family built a church in 1906, I knew I had to be a strong advocate against this behavior... even if I had to stand alone. What motivated this Strong Advocacy is when I realize the power of a name and who named you.

The Church that was build by my family is named St. Luke Disciples Church of Christ, which is still in service today. Bible History help me understand, that St. Luke was one of the four Gospels. Luke, who wrote this Gospel and the book of Acts, was a physician, and anointed writer by Jesus.

With my writing ability, God gave me a unique gift that enable me to decipher things hidden in plain sight. I call this ability, a form of interpretation like that of Bible Daniel; when he interpret **"The Handwriting on the Wall"**. Nevertheless, this is what I discovered about my birth name Luby.

As you can see, my name has four letters like "Luke"; with the first two letters(Lu) the same. And more than that, like St. Luke... the Gospel writer, my name Luby came from the physician that delivered me at birth. The choice to name me after the doctor that delivered me was suggested by his nurse, who assisted him during my birth.

I did not realize, after spending forty years on a diary; I compile into a book, that this book on Homosexuality was the book I was ordained to write. I had to achieve, Saint status(St. Luby) before the writing of this Book was revealed to me. The process in which I reached the "Saint" status was a big surprise when I got there. Did not realize, by isolating myself from the public; with discipline, would cause this to happen. What I have said in a nutshell, is that the mission of the church build by my family was to produce an author/writer like the Church namesake...St. Luke. That is me...Luby Martin.

The Bible says we are surnamed. I have been surname after St. Luke the Gospel writer. *Isaiah 44:5 & 45:4*

Another inspiration for writing this book, is; the fact that Same Sex Marriage has been legalized "nation wide" has caused a great number of ministers to not preach on this issue. I receive a revelation; that this issue in America, is going to cost a lot of ministers their rightful place with God.

If God has "Truly" call you to preach the Gospel; and you neglect to Preach on this behavior, its not going to end well for you. If you are reluctant to preach on this issue; God has given you a way out. What you should say when preaching on scriptures pertaining to Homosexuality or any scriptures for that matter: "That this is what the word of God say...not me". Follow that up with..."and I have been anointed to preach the Bible Gospel." By doing this, you will eliminate a long suffering on your death bed before exiting this world. All ministers that has acquired great following, used, this phrase: "This is What the word of God say... not me."

Now that mega church ministers has receive Celebrity Status, and has rubbed elbows with Hollywood Actors and entertainers; they have forgot how they got where they are. And worse than that, they does not want to offend any of their Hollywood's friends. Instead, they are offending the God who cause them to reach the celebrity status. I have been inspired to leave the ministers with this scripture: *Revelation 2:4, Nevertheless, I have somewhat against thee, because thou hast left thy first love.*

Another motivation for writing this book: I come to realize; our nation was founded upon Bible Principles. There are many signs in the way our laws are written, that these Bible principles are reflected.

As I started on the journey of writing this book; I remembered in grade school and high school, when given an assignment that required library research, it was always an eye opening experience. Why? Because I was getting historical knowledge and great insight from the pioneers and experts on my subject matter. And on top of that, they knew what they were talking about.

When I got to College in doing a thesis, I did my personal fact finding mission into my chosen subject matter as well. This gave me first hand experience in my career choice.

Following this same course of action; once it was made clear, that it was my mission to write this book, I decided to research and go on line and read the information that had been compile on this topic. "Oh...My...God" was my response after reading what some of the renowned psychologist and experts had to say on this issue. They had nothing to say in way of its origin or cure.

On Face book, when I read post in support of this behavior, I thought these comments were only coming from emotional charge Lesbians and Gays that did not have anything to substantiate this behavior. But then, I discovered that psychologist, Sociologist and other so call mental experts had nothing to justify this life choice either. Why I make such a claim as that; because it was so easy to refute any argument I came across during my research. In this book, I will list some of the experts argument and refute them in a way that has never been done before.

Once God gave me a Revelation years ago about "not" taking this behavior lightly, I did thorough research on this topic. It seems that the more people begin to be tolerant of this behavior, the more resolve I became in what the Bible had to say. I was taught, you couldn't go wrong with the Bible. That's because, the Bible holds more "Truths" than any book ever written.

To me, you just know with common sense, something is terribly wrong with a man finding another man sexual desirable. I have known as far back as before starting to school at six years old, that I was a male and where my anatomy belong in the world of sex and procreation. As little boys grew into adolescent, with conversations on the topic of sex; I had a lot to add. Instinctively, as a little boy, I knew girls and boys opposites is what cause natures fit. With that being said, I have to say, the worse "public" thing I have seen in the Homosexual world, is two men kissing. To see that...any normal heterosexual know, something is totally out of sync with nature and normality.

If I was to list the top ten things that disgust me; the top three would have to do with Homosexuality. The first two are so disgusting, I wouldn't dare put them in this book. But number three on the list, is definitely "two men kissing."

To see two males kiss on television, is more "X" Rated than the complete exposure of the anatomy in a Love scene between a man and woman. Even if a child is too young to see a man and woman exposing their anatomy; at least it's Natures Fit...they will eventually understand. Born in a family of six boys and having three older brothers, I am sure as a little brother, I picked up a lot about the girl and boy relationship from them.

I remember on one occasion after supper, the family was sitting in the family room, and out of the blue I ask my oldest brother in front of everyone, "what did P-U-S-Y spell"? Before my oldest brother could respond(not that he was) my mother in her most harsh and scolding voice said to me, "WHERE DID YOU

GET THAT FROM"!!!? For the life of me, I cannot tell you where that came from. And worse than that; what made me ask that question to my older brother in front of the whole family. Today I ask myself; was that some type of test for the future; to write this book? After all, the memory of that event resurface after starting to write this book. I also remember, I was under ten years old at the time. Computers weren't a public thing during that time; so I couldn't blame it on that. And I honestly, did not know what it spelled...it just popped in my head. I did discover later, that I was missing one letter, and can't remember when I solve that part of the mystery either.

I always knew I was a normal male child. Living on a farm and the way my dad and mom worked us; we six boys where normal in our masculinity. Going to Church every Sunday tapered our gender understanding as well. So I feel like I am an expert on being a true male, if nothing else.

Other things motivated this book like knowing that I had a male cousin that was said to be confused about his gender. A rumor was; that he was inter-sexual(both sex organ) at birth, and had surgery making him a male. I have read, that there was a similar rumor of a very popular Hollywood actress who was inter-sexual, that floated around for years.

As my cousin grew, his behavior was laughed at a lot. When God made me realize that this behavior was no laughing matter, I confronted him one night in a Grocery store parking lot. I ask him point blame while sitting in my car with him...Are you Gay? He said he was not interest in women. And proceeded to say, "that is not to say that he wouldn't be with a man if given the opportunity."

What prompt me to ask this question, is that, I had heard he had performed as a female impersonator. My other cousins had gotten together and ask him to perform at the Family Reunion. I thought it was just a gag....something to get a laugh. This wasn't a big issue the first time he perform at the Family reunion. But after our conversation; the next family reunion I made a scene about him performing.

I discovered, that I couldn't get my family to see my point of view, on the danger of exploiting this behavior by letting him perform. So I just didn't attend the Family Reunion anymore.

Its been more than twenty five years since I attended our Family Reunion because of this issue. And now there is a married Lesbian couple from the generation that follows my generation in the family. This lesbian couple has been attending the family reunion for more than ten years. The family that support this Lesbian married couple has experienced two deaths involving a fire arm in recent years. And worse than that, at this time, the murders are unsolved. I can't help from thinking; that these innocent deaths of two family members...one in the mid twenties and the most recent, a voting age teenager are related to the family's support of this open married Lesbian couple. After all, one of the family members of this family, was key, in rejecting my adamant stand against our male Gay cousin performing at the Family Reunion.

During the funeral of the second victim in this family, it triggered a scripture while at her Eulogy. *Jeremiah 3:14: Turn, O backsliding children, saith the Lord: for I am married unto you: and I will take you one of a city, and two of a family, and I will bring you to Zion.* Whether I got the interpretation of that scripture correct or not; God was letting me know, that these two deaths was necessary, for the continuity of life of that family: for supporting this ungodly act of that married Lesbian couple. That scripture said: *"two of a family"*, and that family has experience bloodshed of two members in the last three years. Of which..."blood shed"(*Leviticus 20:13*) is the penalty of that sin.

From these two tragedies, I understood why God wanted me to stand firm against this behavior. The homosexuality of my cousin, was an extension of a Sex Sin Curse brought on by the first generation family that build our family Church.

As was mention earlier, about realizing a curse and doing something about it...that was based on experience. By me wanting to do something about the family "sex sin curse" on both sides of my family; God gave me some unsolicited help. Let me explain the phrase "unsolicited Help".

After I got divorced, God fixed it so I couldn't get remarried. Every relationship for the last twenty eight years since my divorced...has not worked out. The Angels of the Lord has informed me; that by me being a single man on the Homosexual issue; will have a greater impact. Being single and consecrated with a single focus is what is needed to change the direction of this behavior in this nation. So to cure one curse, I am hit with another curse. Incidentally, Sex Sin Curses are the most common curse world wide. Why? Because we all are products of Sex.

My cousin was not the first man that I confronted about this life choice. You see, I am not a person that is going to accept a rumor about someone I know...on this issue. Because, that would be *"judging"*. Furthermore, based on the historical record of the destruction of Sodom and Gomorrah, this behavior carries a serious penalty. I feel, that by me being Dogmatic on this issue, it will help keep the balance in the Nation-World. Once this Nation become unbalance, we are headed for disaster.

A greater motivation in writing this book, is that, I lost a niece in death over this issue a few years ago: a complete, healthy, thirty seven years old woman.

The first book I wrote had a small section on Homosexuality. I gave a copy of this book to her and the family. As soon as I gave it to her, she skim the table of contents. Afterward, she looked at me and said with a big smile, she was glad I mention something about Homosexuality. I told her, it wasn't about me supporting it.

7

Their were rumors about her life style. I didn't pay much attention to that, because she gave me no reason to think of her, other than a normal healthy female. Later, I heard that she was calling around asking all kinds of questions about Homosexuality. But she did not call me and I thought I was one of her favorite uncles. From that, I concluded, that she had read my book with what the Bible said on the topic.

I knew my niece was trying to do the right thing. Because, when I would visit the family I would notice when using the rest room she had her Bible open on her dresser in her bedroom. Then one day, my brother in law(her father) call me and inform me that she had been taken to the hospital. This was during the time the rumors started circulating about her Homosexual inquiries.

She was in a Coma for three days. While waiting at the Hospital with my sister(her mother)...my sister shared with me that a lot of women had been calling my niece lately. She said, she knew what that was about. My sister went on to say, "when my baby come out of this, that was going to stop". Her daughter came out of the coma with a complete recovery and was release from the Hospital.

I knew from this Miracle; she had been given a second chance. My sister, her mother told me, my niece said the exact same words when they picked her up from the Hospital.

After coming home from the hospital, I call her and her dad answered the phone. I ask could I speak to her? He said she was asleep. I told him, please tell her to call me when she awake. Also, let her know, she got a second chance and its important that I talk to her. Four days later, her dad call me and said; she passed...died. My very first thought was, that God took her, to keep her from making this mistake.

If I was going to placed the blame for this death, it would be to the President of the United States. According to the Bible, any leader over a mass of people, who support this behavior, lacks understanding. Especially, if they are only supporting it for political gain...votes in an election.

While I am on the topic of my niece and Homosexuality I want to express, that I take issue when women get caught up in this lifestyle. To me, for a Beautiful woman to give herself to another woman is a waste in nature. You see, Beautiful woman does not know the power and purpose of their Beauty...they think they do. They think that just because they have a universal slate of men to choose from, that is the only perk for beauty...but its not.

First of all, a Beautiful woman (daughter) is a measurement of the greatness that lie in the heart of their Father. I drew this conclusion, by studying great men of the Bible and what it said about the beauty of their daughters. I reference the Bible book of Job at the end of his suffering *Job 42:15* for this theory. I also notice this in history of great men and their daughters, in the world of today.

I believe a woman's beauty is a motivating tool for man to achieve his greatest desire. The Beauty of a woman is also a reward for men that has already achieve greatness. Men like to call them "Trophy Wives".

God gave great men of the Bible Beautiful woman for wives. If you doesn't believe this, consider the affect Bible Rachel had on Bible Jacob in the book of *Genesis* when their eyes first met. The greatest "Love at first sight" story of all times.

When Jacob first saw Rachel, he agreed *to work for her father seven years(Genesis 29:18)* for her hand in marriage...without reservation nor negotiation. But actually, he ended up working fourteen years...just because she was so beautiful. Also, consider his grand father...Bible Abraham, who believe that his wife Sarah was so beautiful that he lied to a king and said she was his sister instead his wife. Just to keep the king from killing him and making Sarah his wife. (Never quiet understood that logic)

Because of these Bible events, I believe that God acts today in our Beauty Contest. Beauty Pageants local, state, national and Miss Universe represent the Greatness of those people in those places. And the woman whose Beauty is based on truth, honesty and love...wins.

I am trying to impress upon the ladies, how important she is to her male counterpart. She is not just a piece of meat...sex partner to be ravished by another woman...as Lesbian relationships goes. Her beauty in her husband eyes is just as much motivation as her encouraging words. Let's not forget the old saying, "Beauty is in the eyes of the beholder". But why....a man behold this beauty? Because it inspires and motivates him.

I have to say, there is something inherently wrong with any woman that has obtain fame with her beauty, to allow another woman to talk her out of *the natural use of her body(Romans 1:26)*. When I read the tabloids about beautiful women or actresses that are lesbian or Bisexual; they drops about three to four points when she rates a Beauty ten. She goes from being Beautiful, to just being cute or pretty.

Beauty comes from within...*Greater is he that is within you, than he that is in the world(John 4:4)*. That beauty is from God. The Beauty from within solidify the external "Pretty". But if there is no internal Beauty, the external pretty is short lived. Those ladies that possess that internal Beauty are those ladies that still look beautiful in their 50's 60's 70's or older. On the other hand, the part of the above scripture that says... *"than he that is in the world"*...is referring to "pretty".

Pretty is what the World sees. And trust me, pretty lesbian and bisexual women, you can loose that God given beauty over night. We call this in our society of today as "aging horribly". Giving yourself to another woman, is an evil within...transformed eventually, externally; as UGLY! What's on the inside, will eventually show up on the outside.

A White woman a few decades ago, made this observation statement to me; that Black woman age better than White woman, because of their skin tone. I told her that skin tone had nothing to do with that, it was that "witch" you had created within. And after the age of thirty; this "witch" within, will start to manifest to the outside. And furthermore, I have seen Black woman that age horribly. I must add, they were mean as the Devil as well.

I've seen plenty of White woman that are not Hollywood's stars in their 50's and 60's that are absolutely Beautiful. And when you talk with them, their beauty comes from a very kind heart. *Proverbs 31* calls them the virtuous woman.

Do you realize, if you allow a member of the same gender to talk you out of the natural use of your body, you can be talked... into...or out of...anything in world? Because...being talked out of the natural use of your body by a member of the same sex; is the same as being talked out your soul by the DEVIL. This is the same Spirit that talked "Eve in the Garden of Eden" into biting the forbidden fruit. And Homosexuality is definite, a "forbidden fruit".

Being talked out of the natural use of your body means you can be talked in to committing crimes like Armed robbery, kidnapping, murder etc. It has happened!!! And furthermore, to be talked out of the natural use of your body by a member of the same sex is worse than "Stockholm Syndrome".

I look at homosexuality as I look at the evil of a snake. I have learn the origin of a snake with its vileness and its evil foundation. A snake can be curled up, just enjoying the warm of the sun on a beautiful summer day doing no one no harm. Because of its history, when I see it, my only impulse is to rid it from the face of the earth. When anything has a history of being the vilest of all creature(Snake) both of animal and human I will treat it with the like. You can look at a snake and just know from how hideous it is design, that it portraits ultimate evil.

When it comes to Homosexuals, especially a man, their present produce an unusual atmosphere to me. I know for a mental condition to be given to a man causing him to desire another man; has to be born out of a very dark place. It can only come from a source of total evil like that of a snake. And I know for the most part; a "Gay" man means no harm...in his mind; like the snake curled up doing no harm. Although I may kill a snake, a Gay man on the other hand, I will move out of his presents. Not that I am afraid of him...its just that male Homosexuals creep me out. I don't want to be close to that kind of evil that make a man think this way. I will only deal with him professionally; and if I can avoid professional contact; I will. You see, I don't know what has cause some of the most masculine men of the world to be turned to this; so I am not going to take any chances. Call me Homophobia if you like. One thing for sure, I have plenty of company. I can only "sympathize" with a Gay man, but I will never be able to "empathize" with him.

The one thing I am sure of; is that, this behavior has evolved from something very evil. And no one is going to talk me into tolerating or putting up with anything that is totally against the laws of Nature and God

If I run into a woman that is Lesbian; I will tolerate her a little more. Not that I think I can change her, but she is natures fit for me...the female. If she is Bisexual, she is confused, and is sister to the Nymphomaniac.

The consequences of allowing the overt acceptance of Homosexual behavior on a National level, is another motivation for writing this book. I strongly believe that there are consequences of Biblical proportion for pushing the public acceptance of this lifestyle in this nation.

With that being said; of my motivation and Inspiration for writing this book, we need to dig deeper and understand actually...what is "Homosexuality" in word and definition?

What Is Homosexuality ?

To approach this subject matter in the best possible light for all to understand, let's get clarity with a universal definition in the English Language of Homosexuality. There is no need of a definition for Heterosexuality. We all are familiar with that lifestyle.

Just in case some has forgotten what the Heterosexual lifestyle is, let's review for a minute.

Heterosexuality is a man and woman couple designed-created by God to fulfill loneliness, companionship, Love and procreation. Heterosexuality, is the lifestyle that is composed of a man and woman that has kept the continuity of our Species in existent for thousands of years through reproduction. Heterosexuality makes for an indefinite existence on earth of our species. Heterosexual is the lifestyle that birth both the **"straight and the Gay"** in the world. This is the relationship, after birth, that both the *"straight and the Gay"* witness as the pattern of Adult life. The Heterosexual is the lifestyle that give a man and woman couple a second chance through birthing children. You can see why there is no need for defining the Heterosexual lifestyle.

On the other hand, Homosexuals is the group needing lots of understanding. The relationship that cannot provide a society with a future. This is the lifestyle that has no equipment to produce another Gay and definite not a Straight(Normal) human being with their Same Sex partner. This is the lifestyle that usually has a short life. Any long life of a Gay is only because they live amongst Heterosexuals as we will prove. Homosexuals are that group that many Heterosexuals are concern whether there will be a society on tomorrow when they get out of bed. Of course, in our society of today, Homosexual is referred as one desiring the Same Sex.

By now, we get the picture of what a Homosexual is. But before defining Homosexuality; let's talk about those who take the first step of admitting that they are Gay.

Homosexuality is the only "UN-natural" behavior once confessed, wants their behavior to be condoned. The Drug Additives, Alcoholics, Addictive Gamblers, child molesters, sex offenders of all kinds etc: are behavior that's not condoned when confessed.

There are many bad habits and addictions that people frowned on that are not good for the family or society. Like Homosexuality, these are addictions and diseases that are formulated in the mind. And when all whom have these unnatural curses and conditions confess; normally, that's protocol in seeking help for healing. And yet, the Homosexual, when they confess their behavior, they wants public acceptance and approval. Also, want Government support to continue it. If its not a problem, why confess to start with? If it is such a normal thing, why is a Homosexual confession camouflage, as "coming out of the closet"? Its the same as any other unfortunate curse that a person been saddle with.

When a Homosexual confesses or come out of the closet; it is like saying to the Alcoholic, now that you have confess this to us(Alcoholic Anonymous) we want everyone here to bring their favorite booze to celebrate his honesty at our next AA meeting.

But some who is reading this will say; Homosexuality is not the same. Oh...but it is. Because, Homosexuality is about sexual obsession in a lewd and disgusting manner; with the Same Sex. Also, fleshly lust is an addiction amongst Heterosexual as well. And after a person has been in a Heterosexual relationship, God help you if you ever get caught in a Homosexual relationship... there is not much hope. Why, because Satan is the father of addictions as well as lies. And he is not going to let you go easily.

So let's get some background information on this very controversial subject called "Homosexuality".

It is said that the term Homosexual was coined in the late 19th century by a German Psychologist Karely Maria Benkert. By syllabicating Homosexual..."Homo" by definition means "same" and "sex(ual)" is self explanatory. Putting the break down definition together, we get the modern day version of "Same Sex" couples.

However, the term Homosexuality by googling is said to mean *a romantic attraction... sexual attraction...or sexual behavior between members of the same sex or gender.* With the word "romantic" in this definition, it is said to mean love.

In this book I have included anyone that does not except their birth anatomy as a Homosexual. This includes: Gays, Lesbian, Bisexual, transgender, cross dressers etc(LGBTC-D). All of which are condemned by the Bible.

When I go back to when Homosexuality was under a little more control with the "Hush Hush" stigma fifty years or more ago, it is a one statement definition. An old "Funk and Wagner" dictionary on my book shelve defined Homosexual as a sexual attraction between members of the same sex. The word "romantic" was added to promote the Same Sex agenda as the same type of Love between a man and woman.

Note: This little exercise of "Googling" verses "old school dictionary" research, is to show how modern day terms, are changing old and pioneers definition; to take us farther away from the path of the Godly.

If Homosexuality is about love, let us dispose of supposition that this is referring to the same type of love between a man and woman. Because, there are many types of love that does not suggest sex. The Homosexual and their supporters says "Love is Love". That is true. But Love is expressed in differ ways in differ types of relationships.

Under "normal conditions" a father does not express his love to his son or daughter the way he express it to his wife. A mother does not express her love to her daughter and son the same as she does her husband. Two brothers does not express their love to each other as they would their wife and neither does two sisters their husbands. The list can go on and on of how love is administer in different ways with differ human relationships.

I will admit, that there is an attraction between two men that can bring them very close. Right off the top of my head, a Bible example is Jonathan's love for David(the slayer of Goliath).

The Bible says, *that the soul of Jonathan was knit with the soul of David, and Jonathan loved him as his own soul 1Samuel 18:1*. You can not get much closer than that, even in a heterosexual relationship. Although Gay advocates has tried to make this relationship between the two men a Gay relationship, there is nothing to suggest that. Not only was Jonathan a very close friend to David, but David was Jonathan's brother-in-law(not do that make a difference in the Homosexual world). David was a strict student of OT law. He made that known to Goliath the Giant right before he dropped him with his sling and rock.

Also, Jonathan's father; King Saul was chosen and anointed by God as Israel's First King. This mean, not only did King Saul know OT Law he had live it; that includes teaching his children on the matter. During that time in history, no "God anointed King"....

son...is going to be under scrutiny about his gender identity. Old Testament pioneers understood what the destruction of Sodom and Gomorrah meant.

This story left in Bible history of Jonathan and David is about understanding what "true friendship" is all about. To support this, David's son Solomon left this on record in the book of *Proverbs 18:24...and there is a friend that sticketh closer than a brother.*

The type of love Jonathan had for David was the same type of love Jesus had for mankind to die on the Cross for our sins forever. Jesus is speaking here(*John 15:12-14*): *This is my commandment, That ye love one another, as I have loved you. Greater love hath no man than this, that a man lay down his life for his **friends**. Ye are my **friends**, if ye do whatsoever I command you.* No love is greater than this and yet Jesus died for all of us to demonstrate how far love goes for a **friend.**

Furthermore, in Davids' defense, (really not necessary) Bible historians recorded him to have at least 19 sons and one Daughter, at least seven wives and literally...only God knows...how many concubines. David was apparently too busy to stray from the heterosexual world. With that, let's take some American History male examples that had close bonding.

Alexander Graham Bell and Mr. Watson...in the invention of the telephone. Lewis and Clark with their Exploration Expeditions, Samuel Morse and Alfred Vail inventor of the telegraph and Morse code. These are three sets of American men that had a common interest or connection that brought them together; and made history. All these men had unusually close male relationships. And yet history, has not revealed any impropriety between these sets of men.

The mentioning of these sets of men is to help those that are being confused about crossing that line in male bonding. Maybe your attraction to another man was meant to do something meaningful in the world and the Devil confused you with sex. I am letting you know, there is something seriously wrong with you if you cross that line.

And furthermore, their is something inherently wrong with you when talking to the same sex and your sex organs start to be stimulated. For you men that support other male Homosexuals, you need to think about that when you are standing near your Homosexual buddy. This should be reason enough for you to check yourself. I have heard men that support Homosexuality say, "if he want to do that, let him do it...that's his business". Yes I agreed, and it is his..."PRIVATE"...business at that.

Other than hearing the dominant word "SEX" in Homosexual; you equally hear the dominant word "Home" without the "e". As long as this conditions was recognize in a Mental Health way it stayed in the privacy of the "Home". This is the reason I name this book HOMOSEXUALITY and not SAME SEX, because we are programmed by dominating word sounds. It should stay in the "Home"...private.

As long as we except the Bible description of this behavior as an Abomination; it remained in the home and private as well. But when the social media started dressing up this behavior by using the phrase "Same Sex" they wanted the public's approval. Same Sex sound less threaten than Homosexuality and the slang that go with it. Also, by using the phrase; "Coming out of the closet" rather than "confessing" doesn't sound like a SIN or a Crime.

And now, its is out of control. The Homosexuals wants to use the bathroom of their mental gender identity; rather than their birth certificate gender identity.

Consider this analogy. When murderers are in prison with other criminals their behavior with each other is accepted(most of the time)...they have something in common. Although prisoners are accepted in prison, by each other regardless of the crime, their behavior is harmful to society. Regardless of how many Homosexuals are in this nation with their Gay Bars and establishment: publicizing their life choice brings harm to a society. That is what the Bible implies about Homosexuality when the punishment is *"death" and their blood should be upon them.(Levit 20:13)* "This behavior hurts the general public". Why else would Moses enforce such a severe punishment as "death" for this behavior. Being on "Death Row" in prison means isolated from not only the "World", but the rest of the prison population as well. So think about that in the above scripture of "Homosexuality" and its death penalty.

Concerning the practice of love making between Same Sex... it is not natures love making; when it involve two individuals having the same sex organs. Whatever this attraction is, that bring same sexes together that involves sharing their private parts...it is not the same as Heterosexual love.

To a "True" Religious taught person of OT and NT values, Same Sex Relationship sends up a red flag immediately.

You ever ask the question; why did Moses direct the laws prohibiting Same Sex to the Man? The answer to that question is, because man performed the first Act after the flood. Also, in the world prior to the flood...Adam and Eve's world...God put man in charge. Correct the man you corrects the woman. I believe, in a lot of cases, a homosexual woman just need to find the right kind of man.

Let's be real about this, the whole Homosexual concept is all about perverse and lewd sexual activity. And to a true Heterosexual, every time the word or thought of Homosexuality or Gay is mention, it produces these "disgusting images" in the true Heterosexuals mind.

Homosexuality is all about the physical. "True love" has to do with the mind.

A Gay person cannot be in love mentally; because, first of all, the mind is already confused about the persons sexual identity. So everything else is going to be confused as well.

The first thought of you being Gay is what your mind is telling you about your biological make up. With all this confusion in your mind, there is no room for love...let's not even think about "True Love".

To be fair about this, Heterosexual couples when they meet... yes, most of the time sex is the first thought. But its the first thought with natures' design...the right equipment. When a "true Heterosexual" meets a person of the same gender, whether social or professional, I GRANT YOU, their first thought is not sexual.

When the Supreme Court in a five-four ruling declared DOMA unconstitutional; actually, what that ruling is saying, is that the majority believes, that the Bible definition of marriage ordained by God is wrong. We all know that is a LIE...the majority in America doesn't believe that. That was not a decision that was to be made by nine(five) people.

Think about this if you will. There were only four spared from the Destruction of Sodom and Gomorrah. That same number of Supreme Court Judges... "four"...declared DOMA Constitutional. Based on the four righteous spared, before the Sodom and Gomorrah destruction, those four Supreme Court Judges represent all the people that does not support Homosexuality in America.

Of the four that was send out from the Sodom and Gomorrah Destruction, before it was over, it was down to three. Paralleling that, less than a year after the Supreme Court ruling on this decision; only three of the four judges supporting DOMA are alive. With these parallels surrounding this decision, believe it or not; it put us on course with the Bible. This means, declaring DOMA unconstitutional in America, will have serious consequences.

Think about this....just in 2015 alone, the year of the five-four ruling declaring DOMA unconstitutional, their were 374 mass killing in the United State. Averaging more than one a day in that year. Doesn't anyone fine that alarming? More mass killings under this President than any other President in the History of the Nation.

Read on...I will prove, unequivocally, that these mass killings are connected with the publicizing of Same Sex Relationships.

One of the arguments of the Gay community is that procreation was not the only reason for marriage. That is correct. God's original reason for creating woman for man is because he saw that man was lonely. *Genesis 2:18; And the Lord God said, it is not good **that the man should be alone**: I will make him an help meet for him.* (This verse alone destroys the Ruling that DOMA is unconstitutional.) Because the procreation part of Man and woman came after the first sin.

That scripture even suggest, if you are not looking for a romantic partner...just a friend...it is best to have the opposite sex as well. That make sense; by choosing the opposite sex as a friend you get both the male and female point of view on any topic. Also, I think, another rationale is that, best friends can cross that line of falling in love. That has happen a lot in the world of today between men and women friendships. So find you an opposite sex person to be a true friend as well.

In the chapter on the creation of the woman for man, it talks about how God used Adam's rib for that purpose. Then God said, that they would be one. So God designed man and woman's sexual parts to fit properly to become one. And throughout the marriage, when disagreement between husband and wife would come about...the couple will make up. The social term for that part of relationships is universally known today as "Make up Sex".

"Make up sex" usually start with facing each other with a kiss. This is symbolic of facing the issue that cause the disagreement. Then it connects with the sexual part design to fit each other, creating the oneness without them never having stop kissing. The sexual part can be access frontal, just like the kissing part of love making. This means that the couple, not only face the problem in kissing, but they have con(front)ed all the issues that led to the disagreement to begin with. Then the motion that is carry out through Sex reminds them of what marriage is all about...give and take-give and take-give and take...etc. They have given this most "common position" between heterosexual couples "making Love" a modern day religious description..."Missionary position".

This little visual of Love making between man and woman, is to illustrate how this oneness God made of them suppose to work. How the whole body in love making naturally interlock between man and woman creating the oneness God intended. And many times; the proof of that oneness, is the birth of a child.

God's design for the marriage of man and woman is without dispute. Let's take a look at why God used the rib of man to create the perfect mate...the woman.

The rib came from the side of man. This put man's female mate close by and equal with him. The rib taken from the side motivates the couple to interlock their hands with the fingers or lock arm in arm(if desired) for that closeness and oneness. This is why the Bible call her his help meet(*Gen 2:18*)...she is nearby if he need her.

God did not take a bone of the backbone, for her to walk behind her husband to be disrespected by him. He did not take a piece of his skull(the head)for her to rule over him. He took her creation from his side. Again, God's creation for marriage between man and woman is indisputable. Whether you view it physical or Spiritually.

Also, with love making between Heterosexual couples... referring to the "missionary position"...the reason this position is given a religious name is because this is God's handiwork. It is said, that the name of this position was created by Christians. The man being on top represent his role in marriage...as the woman to look up to her husband. This was the law, after the "biting of the forbidden fruit" incident by Adam and Eve.

On ANOTHER hand, when a Same Sex Couple has a disagreement and make up; the only thing facing is kissing: and what a disgusting sight that is!!! You doesn't have the smooth transition of sex of frontal connection with the proper equipment(facing each other)like that of man and woman. Connection of the sex organ while kissing(Same Sex Couples) requires both sets (man with man and woman with woman) to have to modify with unnatural equipment and actions. There is no smooth flow in love making. There is no natural oneness fit in the physical.

By visualizing these two examples, you can understand with man and woman creations; why God concluded his creation as he did. (*Genesis 1:26-31)...And God saw every thing that he had made, and behold, **it was very good**....*

I hope that from the definition of Homosexuality, we get a better understanding of how out of sync this behavior is; compared to God's created union of man and woman. To make sure, man totally understand how out of sync this behavior is; he led Moses to call such behavior as *Abomination...punishable by death.(Leviticus 20:13)*

Abomination Verses Discrimination

The Gay community has said, that their life choice is being discriminated upon. But I say nay to that statement. I decided to settle this argument with the greatest authority on human behavior...again...The Holy Bible. Even our eighteen and nineteen century Psychologists use the Bible as a primary source of understanding human behavior.

Moses in describing Same Sex Relationships said that this behavior is an "Abomination". So I decided, that we need to determine whether anti Gays response to this behavior is an Abomination or a discrimination. So you be the judge, based on definition and commentary.

Some may ask, why not explore the difference between Discrimination and Nondiscrimination? The point of this explanation is to let one know, that this is not a prejudicial issue. People who detest Homosexuality are not Bigots. It is an issue, that God has already render his judgment on; through both OT Law and NT Scripture. And with OT Law, he left in vivid detail, an example of his lack of tolerance of this behavior on a MASSIVE scale; with the horrific destruction of Sodom and Gomorrah.

Since I mention the word judgment above, before we get into *Abomination"* verses *"Discrimination* we need to clear up another term that is being tossed around concerning the Homosexual topic. That word is "Judging".

By definition, judging is formulating an opinion: and in this case, usually without facts. If he or she has declared that they are Gay, you doesn't have to form an opinions; they confessed to it...you are not "judging". The most powerful scripture on the Homosexual topic... *Leviticus 20:13 says, If a man also lie with mankind, as he lieth with a woman, both of them have committed an abomination: they shall surely be put to death: their blood shall be upon them.* That scripture, "is" the "Judgment" on Homosexuals. Admission... to the Homosexual lifestyle, sentence you to the penalty in that scripture.

Moses, the author of the "above" *Leviticus* scripture and far most authority on OT law do know the difference between *Abomination* and *Discrimination*. Because, he had dealings with both...*discrimination*...on a personal level. Since we introduce the above Same Sex scripture, declaring that lifestyle an *Abomination;* let's start with that term first.

In the Bible when looking up the law against Same Sex Relationship the punishment that is administer on this behavior is "Death". This punishment is always preceded with the word Abomination. Quoting from a KJV of the OT in the book of *Leviticus 18:22 Thou shalt not lie with mankind, as with womankind: it is Abomination.* Why such a strong word...ABOMINATION?

Moses wrote that commandment. And the way Moses saw it...is the way God saw it. When something is view as an "Abomination", the definition says; *"it is a thing that causes disgust or hatred".* The definition goes on to list a number of synonyms to give clearer understanding as what is meant. Look at the list of words that describe Same Sex Relationships as an *"Abomination"*... *disgrace, horror, detestation, loathing, aversion, revulsion* and the list just goes on and on. I have heard some of these same words used in a casual conversation with heterosexual describing this behavior.

What is interesting, is that, two chapters over from *Leviticus(18:22)* this behavior was repeated with a stronger warning with a consequence. This is found in *Leviticus 20:13* introduce above which says, *If a man also lie with mankind, as he lieth with a woman, both of them have committed an abomination: they shall surely be put to death; their blood shall be upon them.*

In the verse *Leviticus 20:13* it ends with the phrase, *"their blood shall be upon them"*. That phrase means that you bought this punishment on "Yourself". Ponder that a while...if you would. This goes with the "judgment" mention above.

There are NO Government enforce punishments for Homosexuality in the society of today. However, there are punishments for this behavior in some form.

Take AIDS for example: first discovered in Homosexuals and then it drifted in the Heterosexual community. I question that dreadful turn. Why? What I came up with; if Heterosexual are going to support this behavior...they will receive a like punishment. Let me prove that.

In the days of Sodom and Gomorrah's destruction, their were only four people spared. That was Lot, his wife and their two daughters. When the Angel send them out to spare them from that horrific destruction, he gave them one charge and that was; "don't look back". *Genesis 19:17-26....Escape for thy life; **look not behind thee**,...But his wife looked back from behind him, and she became a pillar of salt.* This "salt statue" was similar to ashes left after the destruction of the inhabitants of Sodom and Gomorrah.

For her to look behind her, disobeying an Angels' warning; when she heard the destruction of Sodom and Gomorrah meant that she was connected to and supported those people. The message that was left in the salt statue as a result of her looking back, is that, her action of *"turning around"* meant that she had been *"turned"*. She just hadn't gotten around to participating in that behavior. Like the old saying, "a picture is worth a thousand words...so is this Salt Statue of Lot's wife...one of those words are *"Turned"*.

The word *"Turned"* is a term used in the Gay community of today. This term describe those who had been coach and talked into becoming Gay. Just because...the English Language modern day word *"Turned"*; was used to describe the cause of that Salt Statue...is proof enough, that it was left for all that support this life choice and behavior of TODAY! That Salt Statue is saying, "you that *support* Homosexuality has a like fate with them that practice this behavior".

The danger of a Heterosexual supporting and associating with a Homosexual, is that, there is great temptation to be drawn into that Evil. Especially, if Alcohol and drugs are involved.

While we are defining the word Abomination, let's talk about our sitting President name and position. Being at the Pinnacle of power in this nation and with his open support of Same Sex Relationship; his Presidency created a Homonym: *Obama Nation- Abomination.*

Both words-phrase sound alike and each have "eleven letters" in them. His name Obama has two a's like Abomination. And when you add "nation" to Obama you pick up the second "o" in Abomination. Making the sound and spelling of both the word and phrase equal. Giving both phrase and word equal impact when pronounce.

The President's name and position actually created Moses strong description of this behavior(as a Homonym) *"Abomination... Obama nation"*. With that, President Obama not only supports this behavior; but his name and position (homonym title) described its *disgust* and *hatred*(according to definition). Which will suggest, the doom that goes with this behavior.

Believe it or not, the homonym created from Obama's name and position over this nation, is what makes him completely comfortable in support of this behavior. Not on a conscience level, but subconscious. Let me explain.

When Obama was elected President, he was describe as *"Americans' first African-American President"*. After being over the Nation the first four years, his name grew into "Obama over the nation". And when the topic of Homosexuality came up, with serious thought; that phrase was reduce to *"Obama's nation"*. And that's when he made it clear in his bid for his second term: "I support Same Same Relationship." In other words, he became the subtitle of the American People: *Obama Nation.... Abomination.*

What I am saying, is that, his motivation for support of Homosexuality is based on the Bible description of this disgusting life choice...*ABOMINATION-OBAMA NATION*. This means **He approve and condemn this life choice all at the same time with his name/position in the nation.**

What is really shocking to me, in Obama's first term campaign for President, a couple of local White ministers wrote in the Newspaper; that if Obama get elected, we will have an *Abomination/Obama nation*. That comment was written just like that. I push that aside as a very clever play on words and a racist comment at that. But when he declared emphatically, that he supported Same Sex Relationship; that thought of what those ministers had said came back to me. That memory was triggered even more by the five- four ruling of the Supreme Court.

Throughout History, Government leaders like Kings and Presidents has promoted certain actions, just to find out later, that it was the wrong thing to do. Yes, it seems good at the time, but a different leader in a different time saw it differently. That leader eventually, was able to convince the mass, and it was changed.

For example, take the "First" President of today's "Democratic Party": Andrew Jackson. A very powerful advocate of Slavery. He was so comfortable about his position on this matter, that he felt he was doing God's will. But nine Presidents later...the "First" President of another party; today's "Republican Party": Abraham Lincoln, saw things different. He took a differ approach to the issue. He ask the question: "How do I save the Union?" By asking that question, he change the course of History. This will also happen with our present **Obama Nation...Abomination** on Same Sex Relationships.

The fact that, Candidate and President Obama's name has been in the nations atmosphere for nine years, it has shaped our nation with an Obama nation(*Abomination*) atmosphere. That is why, above, I pointed out the commonality of alphabets and the same numbers of letters(11) in each...*Obama Nation-Abomination:* to let you know, why the nation has gone.."Homosexual".

You see, atmosphere, is what causes the thought process. That is why, many, that once believe the Bible's position on this behavior; minds are now being change. Just goes to show, the Bible never changes: people does.

Even your strongest Mega Church Television ministers are under the "Obama Nation spell". If you voted and support Obama on anything; you cannot help from becoming under this "spell". Even if you voted and supported the President opposing party; but support Homosexuality, you may as well voted for Obama. Why? Because Same Sex Relationship means no procreation. No procreation means no future. No procreation of a species, can also send the message in atmosphere as Genocide. That is what cause the Angels to show up and destroy Sodom and Gomorrah.

Note: To give an example of a positive Atmosphere shaped by an Americans President name; reference the book *"The Half Have Never Been Told" by Jolomark Retunah*. It show how the alphabets in the name Theodore Roosevelt, was necessary to create the right Atmosphere, for the National success of the "Wright Brothers Historical flight".

The critics will say there is nothing to *"Abomination"* and *"Obama Nation"*; the two are not even spell the same. But they sound the same. The word Homonym was created to let us know, this was going to happen a lot in the English Language. Who knows, the word Homonym may have just been created just for such a time as this. Because...if you listen to *Abomination,* the word "nation" is loud and clear, with the correct spelling as well.

Think of the trillions of times, the name Obama has been thought and spoken in this nation in the last nine years. The Bible even support this with: *"He that have ears to hear let him hear what the Spirit is saying(Matt 11:15,Mark 4:9 Revelation, 2:7&290).* And the Spirit in America right now is saying, *"Obama Nation... Abomination";* and that will continue, as long as he is President. Keep in mind, the average person will speak a word and a name, thousands of times over writing it. That is one of the purposes of that scripture.

So what do you think is going to happen when the next President is elected, and start cleaning up the previous administration atmosphere of *"Obama Nation...Abomination"*. Let me give you a hint.

As the George W. Bush administration was ridding itself of the eight year stench of adultery and Gay support atmosphere of the previous Clinton Administration; the historical 911 event took place. Under the two terms of President Bill Clinton, the nation lost more of its moral standing, than any other time in history, because of his adultery.

The 911 incident paid for eight years of sin the Nation allowed under the Clinton Administration. This event mark the end of the Clinton administration and begin of the W. Bush administration.

The Clinton Administration's atmosphere had been shaped with the Bible Spiritual title of *"a wicked and adulterous generation"(Matt. 16:4).* This is because of Clinton's Adultery brought to light while campaigning for President and...after being elected the Nation's President. With this, God allowed people from another country, whose Religious belief were stronger and more focus than ours to take us down. All that pain and sorry the 911 event created, could have been avoided by removing Bill Clinton from office during the Lewinsky scandal.

As long as what this Nation does, Politically or Religiously, is not against Bible Scripture; we stay in the clear of God's wrath. Because, this nation as stated earlier; was founded upon Bible principles.

Although we may have digressed a bit in our definition of *"Abomination"*, we wanted to make sure, you understand how we have gotten where we are in this nation.

With that being said, let's talk about how Same Sex Couples stand up under the scrutiny of the definition...**Discrimination.**

Most of us have an idea of what discrimination mean. For the sake of a clear understanding, let's just get a google definition. It says, *that discrimination is the unjust or prejudicial treatment of different categories of people or things, especially on the grounds of race, age, or sex.* This is the basic definition that all understand with clarity.

I sum up discrimination as someone judging you on things that you have no control over. I cannot help what color my skin is. I cannot help what gender I am. I cannot help that every year I live

31

on earth I become a year older. What I am...is what God made me to be(*Psalms 100:3*)...*it is he that hath made us and not we ourselves...*

One of the greatest moments in our nations history, was when we started the process of removing barrier of discrimination based on race. Which over the years, the vast majority, saw how unfair it was to ostracize and stigmatize a group of people on the basic of how they where born and design.

The Gay community has compared their right to be overt about their life choice, as being discriminated like the African American during the Civil Rights Movement. Then they go on to say, that Same Sex relationship is no different than an interracial marriage. That's not so! You can "Procreate" in an interracial heterosexual relationship...you can "create future generations" with an interracial marriage.

Based on the aforementioned definition of Abomination, you are saying, that interracial relationship are as disgusting as Same Sex Relationship. I am sure that is the way a racist would see it.

Did you know, an interracial marriage between a Black and White person engulf all races? The Black race at one end of the race pole and the White race at the other end... with all other races between. This makes a Black and White interracial couple, the true "Power couple". One reason, is because, children born from a Black and White interracial marriages are the healers of the *racial hatred* in this nation. History referred to them as "Mulattoes": but I refer to them as the "Salvation of our nation on racial hatred".

Moses, who authorize the death penalty in OT Law on Same Sex Relationship, would have something to say about Same Sex relations being the same as an interracial relationship. Not only did Moses authorize the death penalty on Same Sex Relationship (*Leviticus 20:13*); he married a Black Woman. She was not only out of his race, but interracial marriages wasn't even acceptable during that time in History.

To prove that; take a look at the Bible Book of *Numbers 12:1 And Miriam and Aaron spake against Moses because of the Ethiopian woman whom he had married: for he had married an Ethiopian Woman.* All my research on many Religious Historians comments of that scripture support the fact; the Ethiopian woman was Black. In that verse, it even repeated the fact that he married the Ethiopian woman to let one know, this was an unusual occurrence...*for he had married an Ethiopian Woman.* This also support the fact that interracial marriages weren't excepted during that time either. Moses understood that his marriage to the Black woman was the "true power couple"; look what he accomplished. He parted the Red Sea.

Also, in that scripture, you see the discrimination of family members on interracial marriage as in our society of today. *And Miriam and Aaron spake against Moses because of the Ethiopian Woman....* For all who are not familiar with the names *"Miriam"* and *"Aaron"* in that scripture; they are the sister and brother of Moses.

To add to Moses marriage to the Ethiopian Woman; some Bible scholars believe that some of God's chosen men like Enoch, Abraham, Moses and others, knew God's full plan for mankind. This means, God's plan throughout eternity. That is to say, Moses saw this day of interracial marriage acceptance; just as he saw the damaging affect on a society that accepts Same Sex relationships of today.

Let's carry the idea of Moses seeing throughout time a step further.

In the election year 2012, after a poor performance in a debate against his challenger Mitt Romney; President Obama appeared on a morning "Talk Show", declaring, he supported Same Sex Relationship. Just to make sure, he secure all the votes of the Homosexuals. After being elected the first year of his second term...2013; is when the media begin to "force" Homosexuality on the American public.

This started with pushing the idea, that their sexual orientation was being *"discriminated"* upon. Because now, they had the highest support of authority in the nation on their side: "The President of the United States". And...a Black President at that; surely, he know about being discriminated upon"...was their thinking.

So this made the year 2013 a very pivotal year for the publicity and promotion of Same Sex Relationship in our Country.

I wrote this to say, that Moses knew God's complete plan up to our current place in history. How? Because those year numbers; 2013, parallel numerically with the scripture numbers *Leviticus 20:13* that carry the death penalty against Homosexuality.

Let me clarify this. I am not saying, that Moses on a conscious level, wrote that verse *Leviticus 20:13* to parallel with our time of the year 2013(strongest push for Gay rights): I am saying, that the omniscience God is letting you know through me, that scripture is a "Sign", that this OT Law still apply today. And..."a like punishment" will matched the sin.

While we are talking about 2013 and the *Leviticus 20:13* scripture, lets talked about the number of letters in the word "Homosexuality"...the title of this Book. This word itself is composed of 13 letters. I think this is one case, that "Bad Luck" can apply to the number 13.

I have always had a hard time getting over the "bad luck" stigma associated with the number 13. As you can see, even Homosexuality in numerical lettering, suggest it is bad to be described as a person such as this.

The year 2013 was the year I lost my beloved niece I mentioned earlier, over this issue. If that wasn't bad luck for my family, I don't know what is. Even the origin of our Nation with 13 colonies may have been suggesting that Homosexuality be an issue in our nation. And after winning our Independence in 1776; from that date to the first Inaugurated President in 1789 was 13 years. If this 13 is referring to the origin of our nation's colonies, then Homosexuality with thirteen letters could be representing the end of our nation. Because, Homosexuality represent no Procreation... no future.

I recently heard; that the last sin before God destroys a nation, is Homosexuality. The prophet *Isaiah 46;10* sums it up like this... calling *the ending from the beginning...* (referring to the nation origin of 13 colonies with the 13 letters in Homosexuality as the nations end).

Getting back to the word discrimination and Same Sex relationship; remember, *Leviticus 20:13* says...*shall be put to death; their blood will be upon them.* That means they bought this punishment upon themselves. If you want to go around publicizing you are Gay, then a negative reaction for this behavior is within a person rights. That include, those who refused to issue marriage licenses to Same Sex Couples...that is their Religious teaching in action.

They are following Bible protocol on this matter. They are following the advice of the Apostle Paul in *II Corint 6:16-17... Wherefore come out from among them, and be ye separate, saith the Lord, and touch not the unclean thing; and I will receive you...* By not issuing Marriage Licenses to Same Sex couples, this is how they are *being separate* and *coming out from among them:* they are obeying their Bible teaching. That is not *discrimination,* but rather, their Religion in action. Because, Homosexuality, is definite an *unclean thing* as the scripture stated.

Prior to the destruction of Sodom and Gomorrah, the Angels told Lot, his wife and their two daughters to get as far away as possible. That can be viewed, metaphorically, as distancing yourself from this behavior as much as possible.

Backing up for a moment, and viewing the three dominant words that describe discrimination; *Race, Age* and *Sex;* are things we cannot help. These three things follows a natural order. Some Homosexuals say, they were born with these feeling and they cannot help it. And with that, by not being able to public display our homosexual feelings; we are being *"discriminated"* upon. But the *Leviticus 20:13* Scripture let you know you are wrong with the word *"abomination"*.

Then Homosexual supporters ask: "what about those born with feminine voices(speaking of men), and other feminine ways that doesn't pair up with their male birth anatomy? That's just it: the anatomy. What do your anatomy tell you? Unless you are inter sexual(both sex); you follow the protocol of your anatomy. If Heterosexual can act Gay, then Gays can act Heterosexual. Its done all the time.

If you are a man with a light or feminine voice, then you might be looking for a woman with a deep voice. Or the best choice, if confused on your sexual identity and live in a religious taught family, just remain single. That is...if you value the eternity of your soul.

If your mind is not lining up with your anatomy, then it just means this is your cross to bear: we all have one. As far as acting in accordance with your anatomy, take it as a jump start to nature in becoming what your anatomy dictates.

Let's be clear about this Homosexuals; the public is not *discriminating* against you. You are discriminating against you. Your mentality or mind doesn't approve of your anatomy. *Discrimination* is all about people not liking people on the basic of things they cannot help. Can you help the fact you were born with the equipment of a man? No you can't. So tell your female mind to stop *discriminating* against your Male anatomy(Sex *discrimination*). Let your mind know you are "Male" because your anatomy says so!!! It is easier to change your mind, than a physical part of your body: and less costly. And if you cannot convince your mind not to *discriminate* on your anatomy; then remind yourself, you are an *"Abomination"* if you participate in Same Sex Relationships.

We mention Hollywood...the entertaining industry, mission on this issue earlier. They carry more influence in our nation than the Government and Church combined.

For centuries, the strongest forces in a nation was the Church and Government: in that order. But America has a third power. They have Hollywood or the entertainment industry. If Hollywood is on the wrong side of an issue; with their influence through the media; we are in trouble. And yes...Hollywood...for the most part; **"you are on the wrong side of the Homosexual issue."**

It is important that we understand why Hollywood has become more influential that the Church and Government. The people that make up Hollywood, are people, for the most part, who discipline themselves through exercising and dieting-fasting; more religiously, than people that flock to the Church on Sunday morning. That is the type of discipline God requires for Salvation. This type of mind and body discipline, that Hollywood does for vanity; is far greater than what the Church does for Salvation. This type of discipline give Hollywood entertainers a more acceptable vessel for God's Glory than the church. And because of that, many actors and actresses are being used by God unknowingly.

Their influence in Government come from their massive wealth. Putting that with their celebrity status; an endorsement from them carries a lot of weight in the world of Politics.

The name Hollywood, is the description that the Church suppose to demonstrate in the eyes of God. In the word "Hollywood"; by removing one of the "L's", it becomes "Holy Wood".

Holy...is the description God is looking for, of every Bible, true believer.(*I Peter 1:16*) Holy Wood...is what the Cross became; after Jesus death, burial and resurrection. And the people of Hollywood demonstrate a form of this suffering and discipline when they exercise, diet and fast consistently...making for a type of a Church. This is how they get God's attention, and becomes, a very powerful force. Believe it or not, God is please with a lot of them.

The people of Hollywood, doesn't know this, but they make up two very popular Religious sect during Jesus time. These two Religious sects were known as "Pharisee and Sadducee". If you read up on these two Religious sects of people, you will discover, that their description, fit Hollywood...the very rich and powerful sect of OT Religious people. If that is not convincing enough, observe the following interpretation of Pharisee and Sadducee.

When you pronounce "Pharisee": you get the sound of "Fair to see". Doesn't this describe models and actors that are "fair or pleasant to look upon"? And take the word "Sadducee": you hear and see through pronunciation the phrase *"Seduce and See"*. Isn't that what Hollywood does on Television, when acting and inserting commercial of their sponsors products.....*seduce you to see* with their *fair to see* appearance.

During Jesus earthly pilgrimage, he had a lot of problems with the Pharisee and Sadducee. And now with Hollywood strong influence on the media: in like manner of today; these *"Fair to see"*(Pharisee) and "Seduce and see"(Sadducee); are the driving force behind Homosexuality in our nation. In return, violating both OT Law and NT scripture on this issue. Making them a problem with Jesus Christ today as well. Not to mention, how powerful of influence they had on the Legalization of Same Sex Marriage in the Government. Through the media, they are the ones that are promoting the idea of discrimination. Just goes to show, as an actor/actress speaking a word clearly, is more important than understanding its definition.

Another group of people that was associated with the Sadducee and Pharisees were Scribes. Scribes go with Pharisee like Script goes with an Actor....and for good reason. Jesus always referred to Scribes and Pharisees as one group when teaching his disciples. The Scribes were interpreters of the OT Scriptures. Using the root of Scripture...Script; this is the greatest tool of an actor/actress. This makes for a stronger argument that the Hollywood Actors/Actresses are our modern day NT Sadducees, Scribes and Pharisees.

By forcing Homosexuality on their television viewers; the modern day Scribes and Pharisees....Hollywood; are still a problem with Jesus Christ disciples of today. Jesus uses the phrase, *"Woe unto you Scribes and Pharisees"* in the *Matthew 23rd* chapter several times. This same phrase can be applied to the modern day Scribes and Pharisees...Hollywood; for them being the driving force behind Homosexuality. The *Matthew 23rd* chapter also makes a good comparison of Hollywood Actors and Actresses being the modern day version of Scribes and Pharisees. I inserted this information in this book, so Hollywood would know where they fit in the scheme of things in modern day America. They have a form of Godliness but denying the power thereof *(II Timothy 3:5)*.

Being a consistent watcher of movies and television, I have to say, while viewing many programs on many religious issues, Hollywood has a better handle on God's mission for mankind; than many Preacher of the Gospel. That is because of their discipline. That is why it baffles me, to see Hollywood pushing the Same Sex issue so hard. Some of the wisdom used and even spoken in television programs, are wiser than the ministers interpretation of the scriptures while preaching.

Movies and television producers allow the villain(devil) to win throughout the episode, but they doesn't allow him to win in the end. That is the strongest message the Bible teaches; in the battle between good and evil...good will always triumph.

During the Civil Rights movement, Hollywood was on the right side of that issue. After the 1964 Civil Rights law was passed, Hollywood jump on the band wagon and started making their contribution to the nation. They demonstrated to the world, how powerful of an influence they can be in shaping a society for the good. But now, with this Same Sex Marriage issue, they are shoving it down the American throat without any History or Bible to support this. By doing this, Hollywood is demonstrating how they can be a bad influence on society as well. Of course, we have to factor in, a differ generation is running Hollywood now; as oppose to the Civil Rights era.

At least, with the Civil Rights movement, there were plenty of Bible, Religion, and world history to support that change. Take the leader, Martin Luther King Jr; a third generation minister: the most high profile advocate of the Civil Rights movement. His leadership made it clear, that this was a Religious issue. He even had the name of a fifteen century strong advocate of Religion: Martin Luther.

As mention earlier, no one in the movie or television industries has made a movie of someone being Gay, that overcame this malfunction in nature. Why is that? When there are so many cases like this. This is another brand of the Gay community doing the *discriminating*. Acting as though, there are not any stories about people whom have overcome this malfunction.

One of the reason that there are no publicized stories or documentaries of some one who over came this malfunction, because, they understand how degrading it is to admit to something like this. They know that this life choice is an *"abomination and not discrimination"*.

When the Gospel was preach, down through the ages, with shame and death associated with Homosexuality, people did seek help. Many got help through the Church and got on nature course; got married and raise a family, the way God ordain it to be(man with woman).

If a child is mentally sound, born with a physical abnormality, and surgery can correct this: doesn't the doctors perform the needed surgery? Even if a family cannot afford the procedure, some doctors will have compassion on the child, and perform the surgery free of charge. Also...if a child is born with some obvious mental deficiencies, the psychologist make some recommendation for correction. They base their observation on, what society has consider as normal.

The Homosexual can be physical normal, and perform in society on a trade; making contribution to the world. But when it comes down to intimacy, the Homosexual feel that the opposite sex partner ordained by God is not suitable. Some call this; a "screw loose". A homosexual looks normal, talks normal, law abiding citizen, but then they wants the same sex for intimacy... again...screw loose.

This is out of the norm...a mental deficiency...not *discrimination*. Because...based on the Bible history of man and seven billion inhabitants on earth; his mind has been affected: if desiring, a sex partner with the same sex equipment. You have seven billion reasons letting you know, your Homosexual state is out of sync with nature. And you doesn't think something is wrong with you? So what do you do when you have these "SUB-human" feelings.

First, you admit something is wrong. And after that, you have two choices; seek to try to become normal or keep it to yourself: "Don't ask Don't tell". Because of its abnormality; a choice has to be made. This is a personal and private one at that. It only become *discrimination,* when you try to paint this evil behavior as something good and normal. *Isaiah 5:20 Woe unto them that call evil good...* When you publicize this behavior as something good, is when you bring your heterosexual family and friends in danger.

Listen to what the Angels said to Abraham *Genesis 18:20,21 And the Lord said, Because the cry of Sodom and Gomorrah is great, and because their sin is very grievous; I will go down now, and see whether they have done altogether according to the cry of it, which is come unto me; and if not, I will know.*

This behavior had been heard all the way in Heaven. (And Heaven is where ever God reside). If it is bad as it sound, said the Angel; then we will know. *"Cry"* means making a loud noise. With the media pushing this behavior, they are making a...very... loud noise.

The publicity of this behavior is the danger. As long as you are not making public announcements, it means you are accepting your choice of this, and its no ones business but yours. Based on my interpretation of the above scripture, when you publicize Homosexuality, you bring us all in danger.

In the definition of *discrimination,* is the phrase: *unjust or prejudicial treatment.* If you compare that with the definition of *Abomination: a thing that causes disgust or hatred:* this means, it is not *discrimination,* for an Anti-Gay advocate to feel *disgust* or *hatred* of Homosexuality. Abomination(*disgust and hatred*) is God's English Language description: not man: Letting you know, Heterosexual has every right in the world not to like the publicity of this behavior. This is not Bigotry; it is the proper emotional response for a Heterosexual and anti-Gay advocates...*disgust and hatred.*

Ask any Heterosexual male, that does not support Same Sex Relationship, how much he cringe, when he is about to witness two men kissing on Television. That in itself, is an *Abomination.*

Two men kissing...the definition of *Abomination.* From that alone, this behavior is an *Abomination* and *not discrimination.* It only became discrimination when one doesn't understand the Bible book of Genesis on God's creation of man. *Discrimination* are things you have no control over. You do have control of your Homosexual behavior. ***If nothing else, to keep it to yourself.***

The Government getting involve with this issue definite destroys the old political saying of *"Church and State Separate"*. There is no Law in the Constitution about this behavior. Only the Bible has the most affected information on this subject. If the American Constitution, establish by our Founding Fathers, did not spell out a Law on this behavior, then it falls within the first Amendment of freedom of Religion. Which is being shut down by the Supreme Court on the issue of publicizing Homosexuality.

There is no record of this behavior in American History Book up until now. As long as it was kept in the Church and Preach on its *"disgust"* with a death Penalty; it was treated as an *Abomination*. This made it a shame and people kept it to themselves or within the family.

This use to be, the "big family secret"....because the Bible describe it as something debased. This is why Religious people know it to be wrong. Having to tolerate the publicity of this behavior; is in violation of their *"First Amendment Right"*...freedom of Religion. Also, why supporters of Same Sex Relationship stay away from the Bible in defense of this lifestyle as well.

To make sure we are clear on the difference between *"Discrimination* and *Abomination"* let's conclude with this:

The "Public" Segregation and Separation of Black people from White people after the Emancipation Proclamation for 101 years; preceded by the dehumanization of Slavery...was *"Discrimination"*. This was done on the basic of things Black people could not hide nor keep private from the public; while coexistent with their fellow man.

Homosexuals; on the other hand...a group of people(not Race) that violates the laws of God and nature, by publicizing their sexual orientation; is an *Abomination*.

The word *Abomination* was used in the scripture for a two-fold purpose...to make the Homosexual feel the *shame* this behavior promotes and the *disgust* it represent to the Heterosexual. The Gays use of the word *discrimination,* does not change the Anti-Gay *disgust* of this behavior...described by God as an *Abomination.* That is why this book centers around this behavior as a private and personal matter.

Who you have sex with in the privacy of your home is not the business of the "public" and...never been. And having this sex with the same gender has been condemned by the Greatest authority of mankind; the Bible...God.

The only way you can conclude that the intolerance of Homosexuality is *"Discrimination"* and **NOT** an *"Abomination"*; you have to exclude the word *"Abomination"* from the English Language. Furthermore, *"Abomination"*, was the only word in English Language that fitted the original Greek-Hebrew language; describing people that participate in Same Sex Relationships.

Same Sex Raising Children

If a Gay person male or female desire to raise children, there is a protocol established in nature. The very first paragraphs of this Book laid out that protocol. The Birds of Air...follows it...the animal of the land...follows it....the fish of the sea...follows it and so does all the insects and creepy things follows this protocol. And man whom God put over all these creatures suppose to follow it as well.

This process, we determine in the outset of this book is called... procreation. For you that are confuse, this process requires sex organs that fit properly of a male and female. And if all goes well, within about 36-40 weeks a normal healthy child is born. Again, to indulge your confusion, the two humans required for this great event is spelled differ as well...m-a-l-e and f-e-m-a-l-e. This means their will be a distinct difference in the appearance of there anatomy necessary for this act of procreation. This process is designed in man and woman to be a natural part of their body chemistry and their mental state as well.

So, if anyone...or two, decide they want to have a family or raise children and not equipped to follow this protocol; they **_GOT TO KNOW SOMETHING IS WRONG_** with them: that they need help.

What rational human being would allow their child to be part of something that even the child themselves instinctively know...

is wrong. Making this choice and subjecting a child to YOUR choice is the first sign that you are "NOT" parent material. You are subjecting a child to an environment that is totally our of sync with nature. To do this to your children, demonstrates how selfish and irresponsible people who practice Homosexuality are. Yes, you are a Same Sex Couple: you gave up the right to parent, when you made that choice.

How can the court say that Same Sex couples make as good a parent as Heterosexual couples? With the fact, that the difference of male and female is what create a child.

Guiding and directing an offspring, whether animal or human, is always done by one or both that are responsible for that offspring. In many non human species, only one contributor of the birth is responsible for teaching the young the course of survival. Never *two* of the *same sex* of a species are required... animals understand this instinctively. In the human species, the child is taught life lessons by the contributors(male and female) of their existence. This is the only way they understand how to continue the future of their species. By being taught by those that created them.

Two men...regardless of how feminine acting one is, does not give the visual of a mother to a child. Two woman raisin children; especially, male children, are definite out of God's will as well. *The visual of the male and female parents of a child; are just as important as the creation and raising of that child.*

I thought the whole philosophy of publicizing your lifestyle, is because, its what your mentality is telling you. You received this mental thinking, despite what your family environment was demonstrating. ***It doesn't matter whether you are "Gay or Straight"; both had to have "a male and female" to be born.*** And yet, you are not allowing that child the opportunity of this choice.

As you have already seen, I take issue with with Same Sex Couples. But I take more of an issue with them raising children. Many Americans take issue with how the media is pushing this issue on almost all television programs. That is exactly what Same Sex Couples are doing to their children....pushing this behavior down their throat.

Now the media, is also forcing the idea of Gay couples raising children. I use to be able to watch television program after program on one channel. But now, this behavior is being push on the public, so bad through the media; that out of hundreds of T.V channels, I got to search to find a series that's not promoting this behavior. The programs that I am able to fine are so few I had to make rules for myself. That is, if Homosexuality is just mention; without the kissing or sex of Same Sex Couples, you might get watched by me if I can't find nothing else. When I find the star of a series is promoting this behavior; it is off my list immediately and completely.

I am sure, Same Sex Couples are watching...with their children; all these programs promoting this lifestyle. But the worst thing, I have grown to understand, is that, this unnatural lifestyle of Same Sex couples, is draining the virtue out of their children. They are doing their children a disservice in practicing this lifestyle in front of them. Those that support Same Sex couples doesn't understand this type of virtue lost.

This is that quality of virtue that is driven out of a person when practicing things contrary to God and nature. One of the signs of the lost of virtue in a child, is obesity. When Same Sex Couple drives this virtue out of themselves; they takes it from their children: because, as adults, they are the dominant.

You ever seem a well groomed mother with an obese child. That is because mom care more about herself. This is seen in Heterosexual parent as well. But the difference in Homosexuality; is that, just by subjecting your child to this life choice, means a virtue lost of some kind, is automatically. The flip side to this; if a child is practicing Homosexuality and living with "Straight parents", this can cause death for the child. Here again, because the parents are the dominant. I already witness this scenario. Advice for a practicing Gay child, with "Straight parents that doesn't support this choice"...GET OUT OF THAT HOUSE: YOU ARE IN DANGER!!!

I mention earlier, the Salt Statue of Lot's wife that took place during the destruction of Sodom and Gomorrah. How the salt symbolize those who support this behavior. Lot's wife was turned to salt because those who does not indulge in Same Sex Relationships are the Salt of the earth. Salt is a preserver. Jesus told his disciples, (*Matt. 5:13*)*ye are the salt of the earth; but if the **salt** have lost his **savour**, wherewith shall it be salted? It is thenceforth good for nothing, but to be cast out, and to be trodden under foot of men.* The way one*(salt)* looses this **savour** is doing things contrary to laws of God and nature. Same Sex Relationships and those who support this behavior are on that list. It is mention in both OT Law and NT Scriptures.

To give a clearer understanding of those scriptures; let's take a hypothetical situation.

Imagine this if you will; a hundred year experiment. This experiment is about two differ groups of men. Each of these groups will include a hundred men. These men will be label as "Heterosexuals" and "Homosexuals". They will be allow to choose their desired mate for this hundred year experiment. This means, a true Heterosexual male will select a female mate. Based on the definition of Homosexual; his mate is going to be another male. Each group will be in the age category of their early to mid twenties. Each group will be placed on a tract of land ten square miles; which is equivalent to about 6,400 acres.

Of this hundred men that has chosen their desired mate, we have included everything needed for a growing society: Police department, Fire department, Insurance companies, Grocery stores, shopping malls, Lawyers, Doctors, Farmers; you get the picture. Then we are going to throw in contraceptive in one form... condoms. Since we know that Homosexuality is about lewd sexual acts; we are going to give them some protection from sex diseases. The condoms are for the Heterosexuals that doesn't want the large families; and it will make things equal with both groups. We want this situation to follow Bible protocol. That is, the man was created first by God. It was man that God left in charge. That is why the only form of contraception are condoms...leaving the woman free of Birth control.

So after this Hundred year experiment; what are you going to find? Let's visit the Heterosexual community first. During this hundred year period, at least four generation of children were born. Taking an average number of three children born to the original one hundred families and three children born to every family created after that. The population that remains, after subtracting the death toll, still ranges in the tens of thousands. A well progressed city; that has been striving now for one hundred years. They just had their first Centennial Celebration.

Now let's visit the Homosexual tract of land. The first thing we see when we get to the land site, is vines has cover most of the buildings. The streets and asphalt roads has been grown over with grass; with trees in some cases. Walking through grassy, briers and trees, we discovered the cemetery. We notice one grave had five skeleton forms laying beside it. After examining those skeleton forms, an autopsy revealed that there were traces of strychnine discovered in each of the skeleton remains. The conclusion was, that the last five survivals decided to take their life. The last grave was marked 49 years into the 100 year project.

This hypothetical situation was suppose to illustrate what happens when *the salt has lost it savor*, but instead, it gives clarity when there is no salt: salt being the Heterosexuals. Other factors weren't including in the above experiment. Like the laughter of children.

As a parent, when my wife and I was going through hard times; to hear the children laugh in the home was so encouraging. The very existence of children in a community gives you hope. This is why Same Sex couples want to raise children, because children gives off an energy of hope. With the very rich homosexuals; wealth is their form of hope, but no future lineage.

Forty nine years was really being over generous in the above hypothetical experiment for Homosexuals. The Same Sex lifestyle can only last with the support of the Heterosexual. The only reason you have Gay couples living in their old age in our society of today, is because, they are draining from Heterosexuals. Put on a separate land by themselves; life is short...VERY SHORT!

I hope the above hypothetical situation illustrated; simply put, there is no future without the "tools to procreate". Not only is procreation necessary for the continuity of a species, but the atmosphere it generates is just as important. Procreation produces a positive atmosphere that generates a future, and not an end. The very present of an all Same Sex society spells out in the atmosphere; no procreation...no future; resulting in, No Hope.

Listen to what the Angel that destroyed Sodom and Gomorrah said unto Lot. *Genesis 19:22 Haste thee, escape thither; for I cannot do any thing till thou be come thither.* Reading prior verses to that scripture; Lot is debating with the Angels, of where he should go from the destruction that is about to take place. The Angels were telling Lot, to go where he think is safe: because, they couldn't destroyed Sodom and Gomorrah until the Righteous was gone*(thither)*.

One of the reason God destroyed Sodom and Gomorrah, because the inhabitant had no future anyway. The other reason... this curse was spreading in surrounding cities. *Jude 1:7 Even as*

Sodom and Gomorrah, **and the cities about them in like manner,** *giving themselves over to fornication, and going after strange flesh,...*

As the above hypothetical situation demonstrated. The Angels that destroyed the inhabitants of Sodom and Gomorrah were actually doing them a favor. It was probably Lot's prayer that was answered, for the Angels to arrived anyway. As discussed earlier, Lots wife was about to partake in this life style. So with the above hypothetical experiment; can we agreed that Same Sex Marriages has more than a potential to be a "Genocide" to a society?

When talking about the raising of children; we are talking about the future. As you can see, there is no future for Homosexuals. Admittedly, there will always be this behavior in existent. But it is wrong to subject children to this lifestyle. Because, this is confusing the child. Same Sex couples parenting, will have a confusing affect on other issue in life of what is right and wrong for children. There are no guarantees, that children with a Same Sex couple are going to discover the correct teaching of God's word: which is the Greatest guide to what is right and wrong.

If two consenting and sinning adults want to practice this behavior; again, it is there personal and private business. But, if you truly love children, and want to be fair to them, you wouldn't force them to indulge a choice you made: that is against the laws of God and nature. The only way a child is given an option or a choice is through the way they came into existence to begin with. That is with a male and female...man and woman...father and mother. If a Same Sex couple could produce a child through natures course; then they have a right to raise a child. If you want to raise children, then you must do it the way nature has design it.

If you are a woman...you need a man. If you are a man...you need a woman. If you are a mom with children; then you are a single mom with children...Gay or Straight. The same goes with a father with children. You shouldn't have it both ways. Again...this just demonstrates how unfair Homosexuals are. First, they push this life choice on the public; then...on their children.

We have to understand, that children are going to mimic mom and dad. All children know is what mom and dad teaches them. This is not referring to a child prodigy. If one parent is missing and replace with a same gender parent; this will definite bring confusing in later years. Children of divorced Heterosexual(man and woman) couples, and remarries a Heterosexual, is confusing enough as it is. What do you think a Same Sex Relationship does after a Heterosexual divorce?

Its one thing to be born confuse about your sexual identity, but to purposely push it on a child...well...that's just not right. This forces them to practice a life style without knowing any better. You "Can Not" teach a child the right way, when you are clearly demonstrating the wrong way. The old saying, "don't do as I do... do as I say do" is not fair to say to children being raised by Same Sex Couples.

Although, all children raised by Same Sex Couples are not going to follow their examples....it still sends the wrong message to a child. But worse than that, if we allow Same Sex Couples to raise children, we are starting to poison the future and doom this country: not to mention, ending a family lineage.

Homosexuality: How did it really begin?

Many are unaware of where the first act on Homosexuality took place. The answer to that mystery is, research the source where it is first mention...the Bible. And even after researching the Bible; the first Act of Homosexuality is not a Billboard discovery. Nevertheless, my research reveal that the origin of Homosexuality is found in the first family after the flood. This is Noah's family... the builder of the Ark.

By reading the whole story of Noah and the Ark before and after the flood without seeking the truth, one would never discover the first act of Homosexuality. The rationale behind this, is that, the way this incident came about was so degrading and disgusting that Noah did not want to record this event. Nevertheless, it was his duty to record this portion of Bible History; being the first family in the New world.

Noah wanted to make sure, that if you could discern what the recorded verses describing the first act of Homosexuality were saying, you earn this revelation.

Most students of the Bible know that English is not the original language. The information pertaining to this disgusting act in any language, would be so camouflage, that only a dedicated child of God filled with God's "Holy Spirit", would recognize what that Bible scriptures are saying.

The "Holy Ghost" is one of the major demands of being a "born again Christian"... according to the NT. Many Christian neglect this portion of Salvation. One reason, to be endowed with the "Holy Ghost" requires commitment. And when you do get it, it requires a lot of work to keep it. The purpose of the "Holy Ghost" is to reveal things that are not in the printed word of the Bible...showing you how to apply the already printed word. Also, if man has left things out of the Bible, or tampered with it in any way, the Holy Ghost has the power to reveal or bridge any gaps.

Note: *In my reception of this precious and vital ingredient(Holy Ghost) of Salvation, I had a team of men to help me. My reception of the Holy Ghost came after a real Religious Exorcism. When the Evil Spirit was driven out of me and I being filled with the Holy Spirit.... it was mandatory to perform certain acts the rest of my life to keep the Holy Ghost active. Discipline was a must in all areas of life. Memorizing verses of Scriptural and whole Bible chapters at a time, alone with trying to read my Bible daily; is part of the routine. I have to go on long hard Fast for weeks at a time. These Fast would require, that I could not eat nor drink anything. The longest Fast I had to take at one time was 21 days. The first seven days of this Fast; I was required to go without food and water. The second and third week I could only drink water. When I am not Fasting, I have to watch my eating habits daily.*

I added this information to let the reader know, that the information in this Book on Same Sex Relationship; is being written by a person that follow Religious and Salvation protocol.

After discovering the Scriptures that reveal the first act of Homosexuality, God gave me the undocumented details of what preceded the Bible information. This undocumented information was even unknown to Noah at that time; that is why he did not record what I am about to reveal. This is what the revelation of that undocumented information unknowingly to Noah entailed:

As Noah built the ark with perspiration and exercising his body(*as the first man Adam's curse commanded Gen.3:19*); he rid himself of his Evil nature that had entered man after the biting of the forbidden fruit in the Garden of Eden. This evil nature, (Jesus call "darkness" in the NT) was entering another body as it left Noah when working on the Ark. For some reason or another, not only was it necessary to preserve two of each animal from God's original creation, during the flood; but God wanted the darkness that entered Adam and Eve from the original sin preserved as well.

As the evil spirit left Noah through perspiration, it entered his son Ham. Ham had been named to be the recipient of this awful process. Of course, this was happening without either of Noah and his son Ham knowing it. By reading *"The Half Have Never Been Told" by Jolomark Retunah* it will give a complete breakdown of how the name "Ham" was design to be a recipient of Noah's "darkness"...the original sin.

As Noah built the Ark, the evils of sin left his body and entered in Ham. Ham's body would hold this evil and make Noah pure: as pure as the first man Adam. If there was no recipient for this evil that came out of Noah when he perspired, he could not have completed the ark, nor summoned the animals to load on the ark. Without Ham, this evil would have left and come back day after day. This is the way evil does each of us, until we act on it, or make a commitment to get rid of it. But if the evil left and entered another body designed for it, the evil would stay in its new host and progress could be made.

Many ministers and Bible scholars down through the ages wondered why Jesus would choose Judas(the betrayer of Jesus) as a disciple; knowing that he was Evil. The above paragraph is why. Judas was to be the garbage can of evil(darkness); so the other eleven disciples could be Holy and powerful like Jesus. By having Judas around, to receive the other eleven disciples darkness of sin; as they purge themselves of their evil nature, this help them to get an extra boost of the Holy Ghost on the "day of Pentecost". The eleven disciples were purer than the other disciples because of Judas. This is why signs and wonders were more apparent in the eleven Disciples-Apostles Jesus hand picked to spread the Gospel (after his ascension); than the other disciples on the "Day *of Pentecost"*.

A modern day version of how an evil spirit leaves one person for purity and entering another, is in a Minister's family. We all have heard the saying, that Preachers children are sometimes the worse. That's because, if the preachers children are attending public schools, they are being exposed to the evils of the world. The preachers children wanting to be accepted amongst their peers; unknowingly, creates an evil seed. As Preacher Dad and Sanctimonious mom seek the path of Righteousness, the evil spirit leaves them and go in the Children. The minister's children exposure of the world creates an evil seed, making them the host for darkness-evil. This unknowingly help Preacher dad and First lady mom become more Spiritual and Righteous. This helps the children to be excepted by their peers; but...put a damper on their religious teaching by their religious parents.

Nevertheless, after the Ark was finished; by Ham receiving the original sin from his father Noah...Noah was as pure as Adam before the original sin. As Adam in his pure state was able to draw the animal to him and name them(*Genesis 2:20*): Noah was able to summons the Animal in twos and load them on the Ark. So we know the story, how the flood came and washed the Earth clean: after-wards, the Ark rested on dry land.

After the Ark had rested on dry land for a period, Noah begin to farm the land. He grew grapes and made wine. For all those years Noah worked on the Ark and did not drink... keeping his vessel pure and clean, he felt it was time for him to relax a little.

Noah got drunk and laid under his tent naked. The drinking caused Noah's spiritual guard to come completely down. Noah's Spiritual guard had not been down for decades..working on the Ark. The darkness of those demons and evils spirits...from the first sin of Adam and Eve...that came out of Noah and entered his Son Ham; are starting to act up in Ham.

Now that Noah is in a drunken stupor, and his Spiritual guard is completely down; this darkness will find its way back to its original host. Jesus explains this process like this in *Matthew12:13-44:* *"When the unclean spirits is gone out of a man, he walketh through dry places, seeking rest and findeth none, Then he saith, I will return into my house*(Noah's body) *from whence I came out, and when he is come, he findeth it empty swept and garnished, then goeth he,....*

There was just one problem with the evil spirits trying to get back into Noah; that is in his son Ham. Over the years; while building the Ark, they are no longer spirits, they are formed into Ham's body. Those spirits were now Ham...the person. Ham was led to his father's tent, by the guidance of these demons (instinctively) that were first in the father and now in the son.

Because this evil had formed in Ham's body and wanted to get back inside the original host, (Noah, his father) a sexual reaction is created; causing Ham to enter back in a sexual manner, by the first apparent opening. This opening would be anally. This created the first recorded sin of Noah's New World.

The scriptures picks up from here in *Genesis 9:24-27, "And Noah awoke from his wine, and knew what his younger son had done unto him; And he said, Cursed be Canaan; a servant of servants shall he be unto his brethren, And he said, Blessed be the Lord God of Shem; and Canaan shall be his servant, God shall enlarge Japeth and he shall dwell in the tents of Shem; and Canaan shall be his servant."*

What that scripture has just described, is the first act of homosexuality-incest of the New World...in the first family; with the penalty of Servitude...today we call slavery.

Let's back up in the scriptures where the act first takes place. *(Genesis 9:21-22) And "he* (Noah) *drank of the wine, and was drunken;*

and he was uncovered within his tent. And Ham, the father of Canaan, saw the nakedness of his father, and told his two brethren without."

Although the act of sodomy is purposely camouflage; there are key words and phrases that let one know that something has happen here more than just a layman's understanding. The first clue is the severity of Ham's punishment by his father Noah. *His descendents.... starting with Canaan, would be slaves indefinite to Noah's other two sons.*

When the scripture said that Ham *"saw the nakedness of his father"*...the word *"saw"*, is used as a noun...tool. In Bible days, a *saw* is not use to cut wood as we would say today; it is describe as splitting or parting the wood. In the phrase *"saw the nakedness,"* he was opening his father flesh...the *saw* as a tool....his penis.

Then he told his two brothers *"without"*; this *"without"* is talking about without this evil that was within Ham that came from Noah.

The other key phrases and words are found in this verse: *And Noah awoke from his wine, and knew what his younger son had done unto him,(Genesis 9:24-27)*

The word *"knew"*, is fitted in that sentence to make the recorded Bible history accurate. The word *"knew"*; carrying all the weight of that sentence, is making reference to a sexual *"knew"*: a*s in,...and Adam "knew" Eve his wife, and she conceived, and bare Cain. "(Gen.4:1)*

The scripture said, *"done unto him"*: this mean, something was acted out. If he just saw his father naked(as in seeing through the eyes), why would his father cursed Ham's descendent to be slaves indefinite. I think that punishment would be just a "little" excessive for some one to pop their head in his fathers private dwelling and say oops....daddy is drunk and naked. And dad wake up and say: "your descendant are going to be slaves throughout eternity, because you did not put a blanker over me while I was sinning"...I mean drunk. Very excessive action...you think?

When the Scriptures said, he told his *two brothers without* what he had done; Ham was in disbelief of his actions. The two brothers by not wanting to make the situation any worst... by looking on their father, picked up a blanket, got under it and walked backwards and laid it on their father. Shem and Japeth did not want to look upon the shame and disgust that Ham had brought upon their father. Noah awoke under the blanket and felt the anal pain(***knew*** *what his younger son had done*), meaning that the Spirit revealed to him what had taken place. This is what brought on the curse of Servitude.

When this part of Noah's life is preach in your average church today, this scripture is interpret as: Ham looked upon(*saw*) his fathers Nakedness and told his two brothers outside(*without*) the tenth. Then when Noah awoke, and realize(*knew*) his younger son fell to cover his father's nakedness; he cursed him to servitude.

Because of Noah's Son Ham, who performed this first act of Homosexuality, there will always be this curse of Homosexuality some where in a family. Because, every move of the first family is recorded as law. Its just like a modern day first family with the President of the United States. The media records every action the first family make. It is recorded as History. This was the way Bible history was recorded. Not quiet as much detail as today, because of the many tools of the media. This is where the "Holy Ghost" come in, and bridge the gaps as I just done.

Also, Noah's three sons in this new world was responsible for repopulating the planet. This seed of Homosexuality would travel down in some people throughout time. **NOT AS SOMETHING TO EMBRACE AND PROMOTE AS GOOD,** but as a challenge for you **TO DEFEAT EVIL.** It is like other sins of the world: murder, adultery, stealing or anything that is harmful to a society brought on by evil. The NT sometimes describe it as your cross to bear. This become another tool of evil for Satan; similar to the forbidden fruit incident by the first couple Adam and Eve.

By understanding the origin of mankind...the war of Good vs Evil did not start until the Devil seduce Eve. This created Satan having an advocate in evil; being Eve, and God would have Adam, as righteous. Marriage was already established. The Devil will be the cause of the conflicts in marriages. And starting the second New World, with Noah's three Son's; two will represent righteous and one will represent evil. This would be the start of another conflicts for mankind in Noah's new world. In the second New World by Shem and Japeth representing good this gives good an upper hand.

We mention above, that it wasn't only important to save two of each animal of original creation: but it was just as important to preserve the original darkness that enter man after Adam and Eve took of the forbidden fruit. The reason the preservation of the original darkness was important during Noah's flood; was to see, what evil this darkness would create, in the Second New world. So Homosexuality became the new forbidden fruit of the New world. This becomes the sin for the mass; meaning, a group of people would be responsible for correcting it.

In today's society, the roles of good vs evil is not constant with one gender...it changes host. The woman does not always play host to Satan(as with the forbidden fruit) and the man doesn't always play host to God, by obeying his command. In like manner, if you are a Homosexual, it doesn't mean you are descendant from Ham/ Canaan: you can be of Japeth and Shem lineage as well.

To prove this; the punishment of servitude-slavery was placed on Ham's descendant starting with Canaan. But God told Bible Abraham that his descendant's will be in *bondage 400 years(Genesis 15:13)*. By tracing Abraham's genealogy back to Noah's three sons, his lineage goes back to Noah's son Shem. All three of Noah's son was affected by the Servitude curse of Canaan. This was because Noah's three sons children intermarriages...cousins marrying cousins, to repopulate earth after the flood. So the curse of Servitude did not affect one family of Noah's three sons, it affected all three. This is the same as the "publicity" of Homosexuality of today...affecting the whole nation.

From the above description that led up to this; I hope we can conclude, Homosexuality is a curse. Ham did not ask for this, it was dumped on him and his descendents. And even worst; Canaan, whom the curse of servitude was given, did not perform the act. But why was Canaan cursed? Because the seed of this Darkness had already been put in Canaan by his father Ham. And proof of that, look at the way Canaan's name is spelled.

In the name Canaan, it describes how the first Homosexual act was performed and for future generations as well.

Between the first (C) and last letter ("N") of Canaan, you have "anaa". The first three chronological letters "ana" are three fourths and prefix letters for *"anal"*. This is said to be the substitute for the vagina of Gay men. With "anal" being interpret from between the "C' and "N" of Canaan's name; the last letter is describing its location with emphasis on the "n" (creating a homonym) as in "rear (n)end". If you look closely, at the middle of the name Canaan (anaan) after the first "ana"; the remaining "an" look like it is starting to spell *"anal"* again. This interpret as the second male in a Same Sex Male Relationship.

Keep in mind, that the original language of the Bible was NOT English...it was Hebrew and some call it Hebrew-Greek. And yet, from the name Canaan, we can interpret in English... male Homosexuality. This interpretation just shows that the seed of this behavior was already in Canaan: it was his destiny. For a more in depth look of how names predestine the bearer; reference the book title *"The Half Have Never Been Told"* by Jolomark Retunah.

I hope that you can agreed, by the way the first act of Homosexuality took place, that this behavior is an "evil". It is the darkest of sin, right alone with murder. Because...after this "same" darkness enter the first couple...Adam and Eve...procreation was ordain; and the first born child(Cain) murdered the second child(Abel). This is another reason the punishment of Same Sex relationship in *Leviticus 20:13 was by death and described as an Abomination;* because of the first major sin of the children of the first family...which was murder.

What Ham done to his father that created the first act of Homosexuality; was give Noah back the original sin that came from Adam and Eve. But give it back to him in a lewd and disgusting manner.

In the second New World, with Noah being the head male, this original sin was entering back in him symbolic as the serpent. For clarity...that is Ham's penis as the snake...creating the first act of Homosexuality from Adam and Eve's original sin.

After Eve ate of the forbidden fruit...she demonstrated a lack of control, therefore had to be subjected to her husband. To help rid the first couple of this sin, procreation was established. In the pain of child bearing, the woman would paid for her part of the first sin through out time.

But in the second New World, the first sin occurred, with the restoration of the original sin(of Adam and Eve) back in Noah by his son Ham. Because of this lack of control by Ham in sodomizing his father Noah...his curse was, that his descendents(Canaan) would be Servants to the other two brothers descendents.

Let's get a clearer understanding of these two curses in the origin of two different worlds. Eve being subjected to her husband while Ham and his descendents being subjected to his other two brothers.

These punishment are simply saying, because you did not control yourself..."you...Eve will have to obey your husband until that day when the woman has earned her equality back to her husband. And to Ham, because you demonstrated a lack of control, your descendents will have to serve your two brothers until such day as time deem necessary is enough. In other words, because you gave in to flesh...flesh will rule over you for a time.

What has never been reveal to the world, about Ham's descendents(Canaan) serving his two brothers; is that, this created two sets of people in two different times in history; to be Slaves to pay for this sin. This sin was so severe, payment had to be broken down into two installments. Another reason why Homosexuality is not to be tolerated.

The first payment of this curse of Servitude for Ham's sodomizing his father Noah, came with the children of Israel... slaves to Egyptians for 400 years. The Second payment of that curse of Servitude; for that act of Homosexuality, came thousands of years later. This was the Negro Slaves in America, also for 400 years. Let me explain the slave time line in America.

My research has uncover, that the first slave in America was sold in Jamestown Virginia in 1607. The Emancipation Proclamation(January 1, 1863) by President Abraham Lincoln was releasing the Negro Slaves from physical bondage...creating segregation. The Civil Rights Bill of 1964 ended Segregation. It wasn't until 2007 that Barack Obama announced his Candidacy for President and won...that the 400 years of Slavery ended for the Afro-American. This was the second payment for the Bible recorded act of Homosexuality. A Black man at the Pinnacle of Power in the greatest Nation in the worlds; says, that Canaan's descendent has paid for Ham's sin of Sodomy. The Obama Presidency represented the equality of the slave to his once...Slave master.

But really, what ended the servitude curse forever, is that both President Abraham Lincoln and the Dr. Martin Luther

King Jr. ended this with the strongest sealant of all...Blood. In a symbolic, crucified manner at that. Lincoln in a Balcony in a theater: MLK on the Balcony of a Hotel. These elevation while being shot symbolize Jesus hanging and nailed to the Cross...a crucifixion. Also, both death's happen during the Easter Holiday... that celebrates Jesus crucifixion. In fact, Lincoln's death took place on Good Friday...the actual day, celebrated as Jesus' crucifixion. This make both men death, a martyrdom and a sacrifice on a Spiritual level.

Actually, if the truth be told; President Abraham Lincoln crucifiable death on Good Friday was for the Israelite. Because, the name Abraham is who God told that his *descendants...the Israelite, will be in bondage for 400 years(Genesis 15:13)*. After Moses leadership freed the slaves, there wasn't a blood sealant to keep slavery-servitude from happening again. During Moses time, Jesus hadn't came to pave the way for human sacrifices as oppose to animal sacrifices in the OT. This created the future Negro Slave in America. Meaning that, the Canaan curse of servitude-slavery for the first act of Homosexuality wasn't over.

Dr. Martin Luther King Jr. crucifiable death, with the blood sealant, keeps anyone from ever reversing that act of slavery and overt segregation of the African-Americans. That means, through the Negro slave in America, with MLK assassination; the curse of Servitude had ended forever in the physical. The dark skin of the Negro slave is what distinguish Canaan descendents of today. The start of ending Canaan's Servitude Curse in America was in the name Negro.

The name Negro syllabicated like this: Ne-gro...interprets the phrase "Need Growth". The darkness of Ham sin had manifested as an African first, then Negro slave in America. Through "the picking of the White Cotton" it purge the darkness of the first act of Homosexuality. The "Need Growth" was done in the cotton fields in America. This is why the name describing Black people in America has went through so many changes. Because of the "darkness" of evil produced by the first act of Homosexuality. The Negro (Need Growth) name no longer apply. Slavery is over... Canaan's servitude curse has ended. For more on syllabicating words reference the book *"The Half Have Never Been Told"*.

Not only did Ham's Sodomy create two sets of people in the Servitude Curse. God designed it that two places in Bible History... Sodom and Gomorrah were left with a Horrific Destruction demonstrating his intolerance for mass Homosexuality behavior; as in America today. Historians has said, that the Angels reduced those two cities to ashes; with bodies comparable to Cremation of today.

My biggest eye opener about Homosexuality after starting this book, is that, God revealed to me, that he had already demonstrated his destruction of Sodom and Gomorrah in America. This was the World Trade Center...Twin Towers destruction in New York, we now call 911. The nation was so focus on a Political reason for the 911 attack, no one put together, that this attack was about the public and political acceptance of Same Sex Relationship in America.

Ministers around the nations on September 11, 2001 had already concluded that this represent God's displeasure of the Religious decline in America. But no one compared the twin towers' destruction, to that of Sodom and Gomorrah's destruction... not that I heard.

When describing the destruction of Sodom and Gomorrah, it always sounded as a pair of twins...fraternal at that...as in "Twin Towers".

So the Lord took me back down memory lane and refreshed my memory. He reminded me that during the 1992 election year... Bill Clinton in a desperate attempt to offset the many allegation of extramarital affairs made promises to the Gay community about military acceptance. The Gay community, with their supporters, were being viewed as a big vote getter for the coming election.

Once Clinton was elected, as what appeared to be forgiven for his extramarital affairs, his Gay supporters requested their favor. Thus starting a public push for a national acceptance of Homosexuality.

In Clinton's second presidential term; alone with promoting the public acceptance of Homosexuality; the Monica Lewinsky's scandal erupted. With this Scandal and Gay acceptance of millions...(well over the number destroyed in Sodom and Gomorrah) America was on a road of disaster. Once it was true that the Lewinsky affair was fact: and the leader of the free World had lied to the nation(although he recanted and confess)...this was a massive lost to our Religious Protection.

President Clinton received basically a slap on the wrist for this internationally shame he brought upon the nation. And because of his light punishment; the Nation as a whole, had to paid for this lost of Spiritual virtue with the 911 event.

Backing up a little bit more. A few months into the first year of Clinton's Presidency(1993); The Branch Davidian Compound of Waco Texas...a Religious Cult, was burned to the Ground...where 80 members perished. This was like an omen, for the time in the White house of the Clinton Administration. This was during that first 100 days of office...where it is said, that Presidents successes and accomplishments are at its greatest.

As the New Administration of George W. Bush in 2001 begin to settle in the White House...ridding itself of the stench and sin of the previous Clinton Administration; disaster struck, in the destruction of the World Trade Center...Twin Towers.

I mention the destruction of the Davidian Branch Compound above as to say *the way a thing begin is the way it end(Isaiah 46:10).*

(The way Clinton's Administration started is the way it ended.) Both incident entail destruction of fire. I guess in some way, like the day Sodom and Gomorrah was destroy by the Angels. Some may not agreed that the 911 event that happen under W. Bush Administration in 2001 was the results of the previous President Bill Clinton Administration...but IT WAS!!!

President W. Bush administration didn't have time enough to create an evil resulting in this type of disaster. But the eight years of sin and political corruption of the Clinton Administration did. It took years to plan for the attack of 911 to be the success it was by its perpetrators. Men mentally, conditioning their minds to sacrifice their live for a cause; doesn't just come overnight. It could take months and sometimes years in preparation for an event like 911.

The Davidian Branch Compound involved Religion taught in a misguided manner. Not realizing at that time, the Davidian Branch Compound's "cult like teaching" was a symbol of the Nations lost of Religious values. And equally, the destruction of the World Trade Center(Twin towers), was the punishment of the nations lost of Religious value as well.

The men that flew those Airplanes into the World Trade Center were acting in their Religious Belief. They "symbolize" the Angels that destroyed Sodom and Gomorrah.

After this trip down memory land of the Clinton Administration; my only concern now is: What is America's Penalty for legalizing Same Sex Marriage Nation Wide? "What is going to be the cut off number that brings destruction upon America".

My "first" thought on God's cut off point was ten percent; this was the last number Abraham bargain with the Angels to spare Sodom and Gomorrah. *Genesis18:16-33: Then he said, May the Lord not be angry, but let me speak just once more. What if only **ten** can be* *found there?* Abraham is referring to ten righteousness people, to keep the Angels from destroying Sodom and Gomorrah.

I believe, this is where the nation was when the World Trade Center...Twin Towers was destroyed. Also, ten percent is what God request of our earnings in Tithes. Those kill in the 911 was like a sacrificial payment for the nation supporting Homosexuality at that time.

I said ten percent of the population was my "first" thought; but now that Same Sex Marriage is Law; Nationwide. I believe when the nation population reaches one third of Homosexuality, is when God is going to send some form of a horrific destruction. Does this third include those who support this behavior? This is a question I cannot answer. However, if supporters are included, danger is closer than we think.

Why one third? Because Noah had three sons and one son (Ham) started this curse of Homosexuality...representing one third of the families that re-populated the second New World. And America has become the symbol of the "New World" after the flood, according to the words of Christopher Columbus when he discovered this land.

Not only did the twin towers symbolize Sodom and Gomorrah's destruction; I think they also represented Noah two son's that did not keep control of the Homosexuality of their brother Ham's decedents(Canaan).

I drew this conclusion, from the fact, that after the twin towers where destroyed; historians begin to research the prophet Nostradamus to see did he predict the destruction of the World Trade Center. They were able to piece some of his prediction together, to conclude, he foretold of the destruction. The part that interest me in relation to Noah's two son Shem and Japheth, is the part, that said in Nostradamus' prediction..."*two brothers in the New city will be torn apart in the chaos*". The twin towers symbolizing the *two brothers* and *New city* was interpret as New York. The *chaos* obviously was created after the Planes flew into the Twin Towers.

To back up a little, concerning the original sin that enter man... this is the darkest of Sins. After Adam and Eve's first two sons were born, the older son (Cain) killed his younger brother (Abel). So the first child of man and woman produced the darkest of Sin... murder. The first action of sin by Adam and Eve caused them to experience the worse experience of a parent throughout time... the death of a Child killed by a child- sibling. And this same darkness, from the Adam and Eve world: in Noah's new world, produced a dark sin as well...Homosexuality.

You see, Cain and Abel, the first born children through procreation symbolize good and evil. Cain being first born, absorbed all the darkness from the original sin of his parents,... Adam and Eve...which was evil...in order for Abel to be Good. Just like Ham had to be carrier of all the darkness for his two brothers; Shem and Japeth, so they could be good.

When referencing Cain's sin of murdering of his brother Abel: this similarity in America, of brothers killing brothers were exhibited during the Civil War. We can said that the darkness of the original sin was being demonstrated on a mass scale. This War was about ending the punishment of Servitude-slavery brought on by the first act of Homosexuality. But instead, what was happening during this war, is that, the hatred of the slaves being freed was so vicious; that as they were ending the "punishment"...Slavery; the "crime"...Homosexuality, was being created all over again.

The intensity of hatred that was generated during and after the Civil War, was so dark, it created this curse of Homosexuality on both White American and Negro Americans.

To the White man, with the thought of his descendents marrying the Negro slave, his intensity became so hateful and

69

forceful against the Negro slaves; he rather see his descendents with *the same race same gender...than...opposite race opposite gender.* This deep rooted hatred, created a seed pass down to future descendants and now present generation...producing mass Homosexuality.

To support this theory; one day at work, I ask this question while work was slow to some of my White coworkers. "If you had to choose from one of two choices; which would you choose for your child"? "Would you rather them to marry *Same Race Same Sex* or...*Opposite race(Black) and opposite sex".* When I ask this question, the person would always be in silence for a moment trying to understand what I just said. My manager, a female, responded with "My God " *Opposite race opposite sex* of course". The majority of my white coworkers responded that way; except for one man.

When ask this question to him, he responded with, "neither of them are very good choices...are they"? I had to admire his honesty. Of course that was the way me and him talk to each other anyway. That was the end of that.

Then I remembered...months before asking him this question, he told me about purchasing his son a pair of "penny loafers". The story was, that the clerk said they were out of "male penny loafers": but, because of his son's age (7) and the size, there are no difference in the male and female penny loafers. His son said emphatically, "I don't want to wear no girl shoes". So the father ask with a "wink" to the clerk: "could you just check one more time? And what do you know...the clerk found a pair of male penny loafers. So this man had given me his answer to that question months earlier. In reality, the decision to birth a Homosexual descendant is not by asking the question of choice; it is made by the darkness of Evil in ones heart.

The Civil War victory by the Yankees didn't end this War of Race Hatred. In fact, after the Emancipation Proclamation is when Race Hatred actually got started. There weren't any race hatred during Slavery...the Negro Slave role was established; they knew their place. The Secret organization like KKK continue the racial hatred that the Civil War started. This Hatred was a great influence on Black people producing Same Sex tendency as well.

Yes...this is where the curse of Homosexuality originated on a "massive scale" in our Nation "today"...the Civil War.

If any one has reservation about believing that the "death hatred" during the Civil War, is a big cause of today's massive Homosexuality in America; think about what it means when people of the "same gender" decide to become a couple. It means that there is no procreation...no future life or descendants. And when a person has in their heart to murder, it means to end life(Civil War). The thought of hatred of death on another person, whether its carried out or not; still brings this curse of Same Sex attraction in a descendant. Because, this is "Premeditated Murder" in the heart without the act. So murder do take place; in the lost of normal gender identity. This deep root hatred creates a seed of confusion, resulting in child descendent of Homosexuality. Or... this seed of hatred until death in the heart, could also produce a murder down through the family lineage as well.

In observing the first sin resulting in Cain killing his brother Abel; there is a logic that can be gathered from Moses death punishment on Same Sex behavior(*Leviticus 20:13*). If there is no procreation with Same Sex Couples; there is no future life anyway. The Homosexual serve no future purpose.

While on the subject of Homosexuality originating during the Civil War: it is my belief, that it was during this time that Hollywood's support of this behavior originated as well.

Basing that on the fact, that the world is constantly being change by "pass" actions...good or bad, of one person...creating and affecting the future actions of groups of people. There are

71

many Bible and American history examples of that. Take our subject at hand...Homosexuality, by one man Ham, has created mass Homosexuality in the world of today. John Wilkes Booth, the actor; assassination of President Abraham Lincoln, is an American example of affecting a group of people in modern time.

Because John Wilkes Booth, *one man...an actor*; killed President Lincoln...a righteous man: modern day Hollywood *Actors...a group*; are killing the Righteousness in America today with their public support of Homosexuality. To put it another way; John Wilkes Booths; assassination of President Lincoln, are "the Chickens coming home to Roost" in Hollywood...with them supporting the ungodliness of Homosexuality in America today. By this being the most evil and Greatest event of a Hollywood Actor in the History of America...makes him the representative of any other dominating evil carry out by all other actors in America. You can call this, the negative side affect, of making History.

With all of the Religious, Historical, and World affect of President Lincoln freeing the Negro Slaves; everything and everybody that were involved in that event, affects history; then, now and forevermore. That includes; all the public and private hatred...like that of John Wilkes Booths' Assassination demonstrated.

Earlier, I drew a similarity of Hollywood of today; as the Bible sect of Pharisees and Sadducee of the New Testament during Jesus' day. By Hollywood killing the righteousness in America through supporting the ungodliness of Homosexuality, they would be called Boothites in the Old Testament because of John Wilkes Booth...*the Actor*...assassination of Abraham Lincoln.

As I pondered over the hatred generated during the Civil War, causing modern day Homosexuality; the question comes to mind...is there a way to determine how long it take to evolved a Homosexual?

Trying to understand how long it takes to produce a Gay person, the scripture *Deuteronomy 5:9-10* came to mind...*visiting the iniquity of the fathers upon the children unto the third and fourth generation of them that **hate** me, And shewing mercy unto thousands of them that love me and keep my commandments.* These scriptures provide me with a time line on producing a Gay.

It says, *visiting the iniquity of fathers three to four generation.* This is about 75 to 100 years. This scripture mention the word that generate the darkness ... "**hate**". Without Love(which is God) there can only be hate. Deuteronomy is also one of Moses books. He is without doubt, referring to the sin of Same Sex Relationship; alone with other curses and sins committed by man.

No one knows exactly how long it took to build the Ark. But the Bible scriptures on building of the Ark can help with determining this time line of creating a Homosexual.

The Bible time line right before building the Ark stated that *Noah was five hundred years old when he begat Shem, Ham and Japheth(Genesis 5:32).* Then after this; Noah was commanded by God to build the Ark. Noah entered in the ark at six hundred years old. The Ark stayed afloat for a year, then settle on dry land. Whether Noah's three son's were triplets or back to back births, this parallels with the three to four generation mention in the above scripture. After the ark rested on dry land, Noah begin to farm and made wine bringing about the incidence of sodomy mention above.

Let's be clear on this: down through Bible History and even in America when the Gospel was Preached; generating fear with the death penalty on Same Sex Relationship, it would probably take THREE to FOUR generation to create a Homosexual. But now, with the nationwide legalization of this behavior in America, with the wide spread media exposure and experimentation by teenager...Gays are being created on a daily basic. It doesn't take three to four generation. This was another reason Sodom and Gomorrah had to be destroyed. This evil was spreading so quickly. As we pointed out earlier, this behavior was also spreading in surrounding cities. The Book of *Jude 1:7* support this.

Also, in the book of Jude, four verses down, its support the fact that this darkness that causes this curse of Homosexuality come from the darkness in Cain's murder of Abel as well. *Jude 1:11* says: *"Woe unto them! For they have gone in the way of Cain.* I recommend to read the whole first chapter in the Book of *Jude NT.*

When you look at the origin of "public" Homosexuality in the larger cities of America; it was during the 60's. This goes right along with the Civil War generating this behavior. Because...the 60's marks the third to fourth generation from that time. Today's measure of a generation is about twenty to twenty five years. In early America, a generation was mark alone Bible measurement of thirty years. That would put the mass spread of Homosexuality in America perfect with the "Hatred" generated from the Civil War. This would fit right in with the 80's when one of Hollywood's leading "ladies men" was discovered as being Gay....Rock Hudson.

This Racial Hatred by the White people after the freeing of the Negro slaves created another consequence other than Homosexuality in today society. This racial hatred started the migration of yellow races of people to America.

An interracial White and Black couple most of the time produces a yellow child referred to as a "Mulatto". And because of racial hatred, down through American History; this almost stopped this process from happening. To compensate this lost of interracial children, yellow races like Asian, Latinos and Mexican were drawn to America.

The Latino-Spanish immigration is an act of God, because of this Black/White racism, created while freeing the Slave and post Slavery. If you doesn't think that the migration of the Latinos to America was slave related; consider the type of jobs the majority of

Latinos perform once they arrive in America...Blue collar, manual labor and minimum wage jobs...any type of work to survive. This used to be the kind of work perform by the Negro slaves, the first freed Negro, and 20 century "Colored" people...just for survival as well.

The message God is sending to the White man, through this Latinos-Spanish migration is..."*your racial hatred brought this on yourself*". And to America as a whole; the Latinos-Spanish American people...believe it or not...has become our Salvation. That conclusion is drawn, because of the Racial hatred perpetrated on Black people by the White man down through history.

As stated earlier, mulatto children of interracial couples will reduce "racial hatred" in our nation. By the Latinos, and Spanish migration to America; they replaced those millions of mulatto's that were suppose to be born. And now, America has chosen to support the product of this Racial hatred...Homosexuality; as opposed to embracing our Salvation through the acceptance of the Latino-Spanish people. The short version of what I am saying is: *Homosexuality became more preferred than interracial(Black and White) marriages.*

Personally, I rather have a Latino-Spanish American living next door to me than a Homosexual any day. They know the meaning naturally of God's word of *replenish and multiplying* the earth as he commanded. It was said, ten years ago, every "fifth child" born in America was Mexican. At least, with a Latino-Spanish family next door, hope for the future through child bearing is in the atmosphere. Something, a Same Sex couple can't do..."Birth a child".

This means, because Same Sex Marriage is now legalize, it has intensified the procreation and multiplication of Latino-Spanish reproduction in America. Who do you think is taking up the slight in child bearing in America right now? Consider how small the percentage of Latino Gays compared to the Black and White

Gays in America. If there are many, it started mostly after the five-four ruling legalizing Same Sex Marriage by the Supreme Court in 2015. And they would probably be mostly school children.

The question may come to mind, that if hatred unto murder was put in both Afro-American and White people separate; what constitute an interracial Gay couple? A good question.

You get an interracial Gay when a racist marries a liberal. That produces a Gay child with interracial tendency.

This is another one of my life experiences I can share on this subject. Back in the early 90's, a young lady(white) and I had a strong connection with each other; to the point that we had to keep our relationship at work a secret. At one point, she got pressured from work about our relationship...she turned on me and I was terminated.

To prove her loyalty to the white race, she needed to find a white man quick. In her desperation, she married the brother of her greatest female adversary at work. Soon after her marriage, she got pregnant...almost immediately. The man(white) she married had a teenage daughter that was interest in a Black guy. Her step mom(my white friend) was supportive, but the dad threaten with severe consequence about the relationship. Believe it or not, this is what ended her marriage with this man.

Twelve years later, this friend who now has an eleven year old son tracks me down. She had a job proposition for me. This was to help get a car dealership started. We were a very powerful team, and key; in getting the dealership we met at off the ground. We agreed on the monetary part of the deal and I came to work for her. All was forgiven and we started seeing each other.

Just in case you are wondering, how I know about the details of what happen in her marriage after I was terminated...she confessed all this to me after tracking me down. Her honesty, of her confession, is what cause me to agree to work for her and us getting back together.

Through our new courtship, almost immediately, I pass the first test with her eleven year old son. That test was: how did her son feel about mom's boyfriend? She said..."he loves you". I didn't know how deep that love went...neither did she...until her son forbid his mother to sleep with me. When I realize what was going on, I left.

I felt that her Gay Son was punishment for her not being truthful about our relationship twelve years earlier. After finding out that her Gay son love me in the Homosexual way, I realize that he was displaying the love that his mother once had for me. She pushed the seed of our love down in a dark place under the evil of lies and deception...creating a male child of Homosexual. From this story, if you read between the lines you might pick up another cause of Homosexuality...lying to oneself.

Her Gay son is the victim in all this. Not a victim to the extend of embracing this behavior as good, but a victim because somebody else in the family lineage; actions, caused this "curse".

After the above incident, I ran into a worse case of discrimination and Homosexuality. This wasn't about creating a child that would be Gay; this was about boys dying in their twenties.

I took a new job after the above incident. On this new job I met three differ woman at three difference times back to back. These three White woman, had lost through accidental death, a white male family member. By the time I reach the third lady I realize this was more that a coincident, God was trying to show me something.

Two of the accidental dead males were siblings and the other was a mother's son. My heart went out to all three of these women, because, in my conversations with them; I discovered they were finding it hard to cope with this lost. These three difference women that came in my life at difference times had a connection with me. Only with one of them, did our strong connection evolve into a relationship. It was through this relationship that I discovered a great mystery.

Some parents has been destine to produce a child that would marry out of their race. I could only conclude, that this is done to maintain some type of balance in the world. Whether it came from slave masters, in the days of slavery copulating with Negro slave woman; or in modern day society for some other reason...regardless, it seem like a balance of some kind. This goes alone with the above mention of the migrating yellow skin people to America.

The tragedy of this, regardless of how strong an "out of race" attraction a person may have, sometimes they will not act on it; because of things discussed around them from family, friends and society all their life. This negativity around their children on interracial marriage, is so damaging, that they rather for their child to be dead than to marry out of their race. At least, that is what some of the children believe...making statements like..."*my parents will kill me if I come home with a Black guy/girl.*"

Of course, the average civilize parent is not going to say "they rather for their child to be dead than to marry out of their race": or would they? But, this is the judgment on children because of their family and society negativism on this topic. When integration first started; many parents feared, that their child would be in an interracial relationship. But now, coming home with a Same Sex partner is a worse fear; or...IS IT?. In High School, the only benefit of a Same Sex relationship is not having a teen pregnancy. But for a parent to deal with "death" as a third choice, has to mean some serious evil somewhere.

What I am saying, the lost in death of these three young WHITE men; suggested to me, that the parents didn't want a

Gay child, nor an interracial marriage. So death would be a third option: because...marriage is a major step in adulthood. Let me explain.

If you were destined to be in an interracial marriage, and the course you are on, is not moving you in that direction; then the first step of your adult responsibility has been canceled. So you have no purpose. The earth atmosphere would interpret "no purpose" as..."death".

What's in the Heart determines our personal fate as well as the fate of our children in many cases. And the Universe is interpreting the intensity of your heart like it did in days of the Civil war. The Bible teaches us, that the Heart is God's measuring stick on good and evil.

Going further on this issue, about children marrying out of their race; strikes another truth about Gay men. Believe it or not, a Gay man is really an Angel of God that has been corrupted. Let's look at an Angels make up.

He is both male and female. He is male in his anatomy, but female in his thinking(so they say). The Angels of "God" are men as before the rib surgery of Adam, creating Eve. This means the three single White males mention above where Angels. Neither of the three were married.

If a man is born whole as an Angel, that means, he would not have need of a female. But if he is born whole and raised in a family with a mom and dad, he is programmed to be married. So he grows up being a whole man(let's say white) that doesn't have an attraction for a White Woman. But because he is taught to marry his "own kind"; he starts the trend of many divorces...if they are lucky. This is the other option of the three males dying in their early twenties mentioned above...many divorces. For death to be a consequence of racial teaching, the parents had to have done a lot of damage to their children thinking.

79

As you have observed in society, that many interracial couples allow Love to rule over racism and blood. When you see interracial couples together, you doesn't know; that deep inside, that it was either this relationship, Homosexuality or Death. The couple doesn't know either: their survival instinct kicks in and they know that this is where they suppose to be, regardless of their up bringing or what society think.

As stated earlier, that one big problem of the publicity of Homosexuality is a misinterpretation. That is, the Gay community trying to compare Same Sex Relationship with Interracial relationship. There is a very small bit of truth in that; but not like the Gays think. Understanding of why; can get very deep and confusing.

As you can see, from the above information of what suppose to be an interracial relationship; can result in a Homosexuality because of bias racial teaching. This confusion is the same confusion given to a child whose mental state does not line up with their biological make up. Satan has put a curse on you and your family; because of the darkness of racial hatred some where in the family lineage. You can't let the Devil tell you that you are a woman, when your anatomy says man. The Devil works in the mind. That is what Jesus' teachings was all about...the mind. *Belief it or not, a "True" Religious Exorcism can straighten that mind right out.*

The point I am trying to make once again; is that Homosexuality is a curse, and its all because of an ancestor or someone in your family lineage that proceeded your birth. But you have the ability to end this curse, and *"save"* the soul of the one that started it. That ancestor might be dead; but you still can save them. Listen to what *Daniel 12:2* have to say; *And many of them that sleep in the dust of the earth shall awake, some to everlasting life, and some to shame and everlasting contempt.* What do you think that mean?

This means, some people die and immediately, because of the Good life they lived, they went straight to Heaven. Others, that lived a life of sin, that didn't ask forgiveness prior to dying; have to remain in death until the "Great Judgment Day". Remaining in death...in hopes, that a descendant will redeem their "unforgiven sin". Unforgiven...in that you never ask for forgiveness. You have to ask for forgiveness to be forgiven. Salvation is free...but you got to do your part. The dead's descendant are a Second chance.

Let's get clarity on this; by using, probably, a real situation. Your ancestor was a racist white man (KKK) that participated in the lynching of a Black man. But down through history, a great grand daughter of the KKK marries a Black man. The Great Gran fathers awakes on Judgment Day, knowing he died in his sin; and to his surprise, he is counted with the Righteous(sheep) and not the Wicked(goats). Great Gran dad didn't wake up to everlasting shame, but to everlasting life(*Matt 25:31-46*); all because, Great Gran daughter followed her heart: not family or society.

With this analogy, after the nation get integration on track, the evil one...Lucifer; starts loosing the Battle to God again. Then he goes for Homosexuality. Now that the Gays has been given legal publicity by the Government; there is no need to try to overcome this homosexual malfunction. They doesn't have to believe the Bible, because the Government says its okay. Not realizing as a Gay; they are the last chance to save their ancestor linage.

Their is a Religious denomination in America; that believes, the living, can actually redeem the soul of the dead. It is the Church of Latter Day Saints; with the Book of Mormon. The history of the Mormon Religion is about early inhabitants of Americans, who had their own account of Jesus when he was here on earth. The record of this was left in Gold plates that was not put in the Holy Bible.

The Mormons believes, that you can be Baptized for the dead. Meaning, although an ancestor did not believe in God and died in their sin, you can think on them while being Baptize and this cleanses their sins alone with your sins. The Mormon religion also have a great program on Genealogy.

While on the topic of the Church of Latter Day Saints; I just read an article how the Mormons are so adamant about their teaching against Homosexuality that thirty two(32) members has committed Suicide. That just shows how strong the Devil is against the Church.

For the "nonbelievers of God"; who are Gay...Satan confusing the mind was good enough. But because the Devil aim has been to destroy the Church from the beginning; he is really reaping havoc in the Mormon Church with Suicide. First, the Devil convince you, that you are Gay...then he convinces you to Kill yourself. Sound like a big victory for the Devil to me...the "two in one" Special.

Whether you know it or not, the *Leviticus 20:13* scripture applies to Suicide as well. Let's read it: *If a man also lie with mankind, as he lieth with a woman, both of them have committed an abomination: they shall surely be put to death; their blood shall be upon them.* Whether death is through, Homicide, Suicide or other acts of God...be assured...Death is going to follow this sin...mostly through Blood Shed. Because...that scripture say so. If you are living this scripture...you are dead already.

These Suicides taking place in the Mormon Church is another example, that demonstrates how selfish Homosexuals are. To me, a person that commit Suicide is a very selfish person anyway... who is only looking for the wrong kind of attention and pity. So they take their life to get even: leaving their Love ones to morn their lost.

If the Latter Day Saints are true to their Faith, this does not suppose to be happening. Based on my time under the Mormon teaching; those that committed suicide, were not true to the Mormon Faith to begin with. Because, this is one Religion, that follows a very strict code of Religious practice. This is one of the reason I like their teaching...they are serious about being a good representative of the Gospel of Jesus Christ.

I thought I need to insert this on behalf of the Mormon leaders; to encourage them not to give in to media pressure. The Mormon Religion has endured a lot of controversy throughout history. I encourage the LDS leaders to stand Strong, because they still can fulfill the "original vision-mission" of its founder Joseph Smith; which is...to save America. This will be done, by being one of the largest group of religious believer who does not buckle to media pressure on the publicity of Homosexuality in our nation.

Nevertheless, in continuing on the topic of redeeming a dead love one; if you do not seek help to correct your Homosexual state, you are hurting a parent or an ancestor that has no idea they caused your malfunction in nature. A mother that had severe hate in her heart while carrying you during pregnancy; or a grand parents that participated in some hated action to another person: all, can cause Homosexuality or murder. This is all on you now to correct this.

They will be a day of Judgment...no doubt about that. This judgment I am referring, will not be on the physical plane, but a spiritual plane; invisible to the physical sight. Being carry out by those who are working in the invisible rim everyday we live, and we not having a clue on this. *Hebrew 12:1 Wherefore, seeing we also are compassed about with so great a cloud of witnesses...*

And worst than that, if you doesn't seek to correct your Homosexual state, you are ending the family lineage, and...any hope of a descendent correcting your sin as well. The punishment for not correcting this malfunction of nature, is not only an after life punishment, it starts prior to death.

For many, who receive the wrong guidance about Homosexuality, by a trusted authority figure; a horrible suffering on your death bed can come to you. This suffering help purges the iniquity of the sin of Homosexuality prior to dying. AIDS is one of the tools used as a purger of this sin. Maybe the name AIDS is why God gave the words that created this acronym...to AID you out of this world to a better place.

A suffering of similar form, also comes to "those who support this behavior" as well. We constantly keep reminding you of this, throughout this book for good reason.

The Bible is consistent in both OT and NT on certain sins that will not be tolerated. For a sin in OT Law like Homosexuality, there is a physical punishment at...or prior to your death. This is because the OT Law deals with the physical, to perfect or control the spiritual. In NT scriptures, if this same sin is being condemned; it is dealing with the Spirit of man.

The layman or the non believer of God's term for spirit; is the mind. The NT let one know, that sin starts in the mind. We know the whole issue of Homosexuality is about the mind and it not lining up with the birth anatomy.

The sin that is written in OT Law with its punishment and again in NT Scriptures; let you know, you have a double punishment...on earth...and...after death.

We have talked a lot about the Spirit and the evil of Homosexuality. It is hard for people that are so focus on the physical, to wrap their head around the Spiritual. Even the Television and Movie producer understand this to some degree. This is evidence by the many fictitious Vampire, Werewolf and Witches stories that are produced by the film industries. These type of programs are all about *"turning"* someone to one of these creatures or cult-like teaching. These T.V. Programs are actually metaphors of Homosexuality. Especially, when referring to the term *"turned"* mention earlier. This is probably hard for Homosexuals and their supporters to believe.

People does not believe in the Devil...if they did; they wouldn't be supporting or practicing Homosexuality. But the Devil and evil is real. Sometimes the evil is what reminds me that there is a God.

If a person is not seeking help to rid them of this evil; then they are playing right into the hands of the Devil. The Evil one Lucifer, plans to win this spiritual battle in America; because, we are God's chosen nation of the world.

When segregation was quickly being changed in America to integration; Satan came up with another plan to win the Spiritual battle. He started the process of Homosexuality; by removing prayer from the schools. Of course, we didn't know that Public Homosexuality was going to be the results of removing prayer out of the school. But, with the election of a couple of Spiritually, "misguided Presidents"; here we are.

In 1962 prayer was remove from American Schools. Of which, this act had a domino affect on the Religious establishment in America. President Obama wasn't even one year old at this time...speaking of one of the "misguided Presidents." The fact that prayer was remove from the American's schools; before he started to school, could explain his lack of Bible understanding about Homosexuality.

Nevertheless, it seems that sometime Lucifer is one step ahead of man, but he is not ahead of God. God allows Lucifer to have his time with you individually as person and collectively as a nation. A good example of God allowing Satan to have his way with his chosen, individually, is in the Bible book of Job. There are many example in the OT where God allow Satan to defeat God's chosen people in Battle or War. But in the end, "Good" always win or rather God always win. Good win because God's chosen realize why they lost a battle or war: they repent; then God turn the curse into a blessing.

To be delivered from the oppression of an evil like Homosexuality; individually, or a group; there is always something that must be done before this can happen. And America is no better than any other nation when it comes to the protocol on correcting sin. There is something this nation must do to restore our religion and moral state back.

In the days of Jonah, he had to tell the "great city Nineveh" of God's impending doom: if the people didn't do something to get back on a Godly track. This is what this book is about. Warning this "great Nation America" about an impending Doom.

However, the difference between Bible Jonah and me, is that, if God told Jonah to prophesied a "Doom" he wanted God to bring it. Jonah didn't want to be accused of prophesying something that wasn't going to happen...to be label a "false Prophet". As for me, I...really don't want no impending doom to come upon America; especially, if its the type of doom I think is coming. I rather be wrong about everything in this book, than for us to suffer the fate I have envisioned.

One reason Jonah didn't care about the doom God was going to bring...he didn't live in Ninevah. You see, this is my country... my home, and I care what happens to it.

I am hoping by now, that you are getting the picture, that Homosexuality is a curse upon you, your child, and this nation for promoting the publicity of this life choice. This is not something that is good for us as a nation.

I read that Gwen Stefani said, that she could be so blessed to have a Gay Son. Why would somebody wish that on their child??? That statement alone, shows how ignorant we are as a nation on this issue. The only way a Gay child is a Blessing, is that child take steps in correcting this malfunction in nature. By doing this, probably, help rid a sin of detriment of a mother like her, for making such a misguided statement. Any child that admits, and overcome the Homosexual curse; is a person who will help save America.

Please understand this, practicing this behavior is a choice that one makes. That this is something that is created out of the pits of evil. That this evil is born out of the epitome of a very dark place. I concluded, that this deep rooted hatred, that cause Homosexuality in the majority of cases, is racially motivated.

This Racial Hatred we have in our Nation is a destructive force. To embrace Same Sex Relationships is embracing the curse of this Hate. Mass killings in America, is the echo of the Civil War on this issue. Most mass killings in our nation today, is triggered by Same Sex relationship. Why...because Homosexuality is all about confusion and that's what causes a person to act out and just start shooting the innocent. The blood shed is what the scriptures *Leviticus 20:13* has predicted, when it say;*"their blood should be upon them".*

Mass killings, is why I mentions Sodom and Gomorrah in every chapter so far in this message. Now...in American; we are experiencing mass murder at an alarming rate. These random mass killings in America, is kinda like payment as we go for legalizing the publicity on Same Sex Marriage. As oppose to paying in one lump Sum, like Sodom and Gomorrah. The question rolling around in my mind now; "how long will it be before the Almighty require payment in full or a balloon payment" on this sin.

We mention earlier, how President Obama in his second term campaign, made it clear, he supported Same Sex Relationship. This was key in his elected second term in 2012. And after his second term election, a month later, December 14, 2012, the nation experience one of the worse mass killing in the history of our nation. This was in Newtown Connecticut, when 20 children between the age of 6 and 7 life was cut short by a deranged 20 year old male. Little did we know then, that this will be the first of many mass murders in President Obama's second term.

This massacre goes back to Obama's support of Gay Marriage. Because, at that time, Connecticut was the second state in the nation to endorse Same Sex Marriage. The first State to endorse Same Sex Marriage was Massachusetts. The Governor that sign off on it was Mitt Romney. His punishment for endorsing Same Sex Marriage in that state, was loosing the election to Obama. Obama didn't need to win a "Second Term", his purpose had already been served:"The first President of Color". This was God's wrath upon the Governor Romney, because, being a devout Mormon, he was in violation of his religion's strong stance against the Homosexual life choice.

Sandy Hook Elementary School massacre, was the nation punishment for electing Obama; after he made such an adamant statement of support for Same Sex Marriage...just to lock down all the Homosexual votes. (Is it just my imagination, that a second term is always where Presidents mess up?)

The slaughtering of those innocent lives, carries a powerful message about Homosexuality. Which is, the slaughtering done in most mass killings, with no regard for human life; describes how Homosexuality is viewed when it is called an *"Abomination"*. And God's message at Sandy Hook Elementary was: *"I will punish one of the first states in the nation that endorse this ungodly behavior to get their attention"*. Because we didn't get the message of those young innocent lives taken, it kept happening. The age of these children that was slaughtered had the strongest message.

In OT Law, the greater the sin, the younger the sacrifice of ones livestock had to be. For a bad sin, God requires the very best... young and tender. When we violate God's command, whether OT Law or NT Scripture *"we looses the benefit of our Eternal Sacrifice of Jesus Christ"*. Because of this, we have to create our *"own human Sacrifices"*.

Promoting Same Sex Marriage, violates both OT Law and NT scriptures. This is what all these mass killings in America are saying. The practice of Homosexuality is saying, *"We have refuse the eternal Sacrifice of Jesus Christ"*. To atone for this, sacrifices are not going to be from the Military...people prepared for battle. No... these sacrifices are going to be civilian Americans: men, women and children...unprepared and innocent; like that of a Lamb led to the slaughter...as Jesus crucifixion demonstrated.

These young and innocent lives in mass killings, are not only being taken for the publicity of the nations' support on Same Sex marriage. If heterosexuals are supporting the marriage of Same Sex couples, innocent blood is being shed in that family as well. Parents and gran parents are burying children, whose blood is being shed because of their support of Same Sex marriage in the family, and they not understanding this.

It is true, that we all are not at the same spiritual level. Especially, understanding how to handle a Homosexual person. This is the sad part about that. Regardless of your understanding, the consequence of supporting this behavior is still the same. If the Bible says *blood is going to be shed;* then blood is going to be shed...its automatic. This book is to help you understand why you have lost a child or gran child way ahead of its time in a blood shed death.

Admittedly, *all young deaths are "NOT" caused by supporting Homosexuality*. But there are ways you can test to see which ones are today. Ask yourself this question. Am I supporting a Homosexual or Same Sex couple in my immediate family? If so, this is your answer. Ask yourself another question. Did I not approach a family member, being a preacher of the Gospel about what the Bible has to say about this behavior? Are these deaths involving a weapon or Bloodshed? If the answers to these question are yes...now you understand your lost. We are not referring to childhood sickness or terminal ill people. Of course, these types of life-death situation has their purpose as well...to get your attention on something.

Let's make this clear. If a family is supporting a Same Sex marriage relationship, a payment is due for violating this sin. What I am noticing is that payment is coming every three years. This three years; parallels with the end of Jesus three year ministry with crucifixion on the cross. Again, when the scriptures are violated, we looses our eternal sacrifice of Jesus. Especially, if we doesn't ask for forgiveness and make a change in our life. A family supporting a Same Sex marriage is nothing you can just "pray" away. You got to make a definitive move that distance you from this behavior.

When the Angel told Lot, his wife and two daughters to get out of Sodom and Gomorrah...a spiritual interpretation of that is; you have to distance yourself from this behavior in the physical to determine your spiritual distant. Before this book was published, I had to distant myself from a family member that chose this lifestyle at the distance of more than 400 miles. Which means; "The Almighty" has given me a low and almost no tolerance for this behavior.

What I am saying, if its not clear; if we are supporting Same Sex Marriage in our family; violating the scriptures, then somebody in the family has to be taken for the continuity of life in the family. Do you want to be the next young one chosen as the sacrificial lamb for the family? If not, make sure everyone know where you stand on this issue. If you will examine the nations mass shootings of victims, you might find that those victims are strong supporters of Same Sex marriage-relationship.

There is a reason for everything;(everything happens for a reason) you just got to seek God for the answer. And remember this...you only get the answer, when you "REALLY" want to know.

It has become my responsibility, to convince the public, that the Sandy Hook School massacre of 2012 was related to Homosexuality. This will includes, the public support of President, Obama and Connecticut being the second, of the first two states in the nation, to endorse Same Sex Marriage.

The way it was revealed to me that the Sandy Hook School massacre was related to President Obama and Homosexuality; was the date on which it took place...December 14.

December 14 is the day the first President; George Washington died in 1799. So this massacre is on a National historical day, relating to the first President of the United States. Obama is a first president of the United State: "first African American President". The main part of this massacre on this date, pertaining to the nation and Obama, is that these death has to do with a first President. When you add this to Connecticut being the second state to endorse Same Sex marriage; you come up with; President Obama support of Homosexuality...resulting in these deaths.

We gave the logic of "Why"; the state Connecticut suffering this type of lost: being the second state to endorse same sex marriages in the nation at that time. But why Newtown and Sandy Hook Elementary were chosen for this horrific event; is above my Religious teaching. Other than God's will...I am as baffle as you are.

Conclusion of this interpretation of those 26 deaths at Sandy Hook Elementary on December 14, 2012...the fault of President Obama. Their blood is on his hands. In the eyes of God, he is just as responsible as the man that pulled the trigger: by his adamant support of Same Sex relationship. And since that day, mass killings has continued throughout Obama's second term in office at an alarming rate.

As long as "the powers to be" continue to support Same Sex Relationship, we are going to have Mass Murders and unusual

Natural Disaster in our nation. *Was there Mass murder in America before the Obama Presidency? Yes there was.* But not with this type of consistency and publicity. This is not going to change: because, it is Biblical written(*Matt. 24:35*): *"Heaven and Earth will pass away but my words will not pass a way."* The word of God, in the Bible, has predicted all those things and we are starting to experience them. Through this book, I am informing this nation why these things are happening.

Continuing on the subject of where Homosexuality really begin; lets talk about the most celebrated Gay on the planet... Ellen Degeneres. She was the biggest boost on confession of being Gay(Coming out of the closet).

My research reveal that Ellen Degeneres after playing the role as a Gay person on a TV sitcom, made a public confession of being Gay on April 6, 1997. This may come as a surprise, but my name interpretation skill reveal that she was destine to do that.

Having several years as a successful talk show host, and being the first to confess being Gay publicly, makes her the number one Gay in the world. She is also very comfortable being Gay. Almost as though she is doing God's will. Would you believe it....she is... that is....doing God's will.

It is hard for me not to think about the word "Degenerate", when I hear the last name of Ellen "Degeneres". This is one of those situation that the scripture *"He that have ears to hear let him hear what the Spirit is saying"* could easily apply. I have used this Scriptures a few times in this book: because sound, whether it is in the calling of a name or ringing of a Bell, is a Spiritual process. Sound or word pronunciation is going to have the greatest impact of any word usage.

With the President name and position we interpret earlier, as homonym to *Abomination* (Obama Nation); and the name Degeneres-Degenerate associated with Homosexuality; there is no way this can possibly have a happy ending for this nation. Coming from two high profile celebrities.

By her name being called with the dominate sound of "Degenerate"; the definition of that word is affecting our moral and possibly our physical climate. Although her name has been in the public long before President Obama...based on interpretations; both names are equally damaging to the atmosphere in our Country.

Take a look at the definition of Degenerate: *having lost the physical, mental, or moral qualities* __*considered normal*__ *and desirable showing evidence of decline.* That could be talking about the Ozone layer. This is what the sound of her name is doing to the Atmosphere. The single word definition of "degenerate" includes, *debased, degraded, corrupt, impure*...all of which can go alone with synonyms of *Abomination*. Making the publicity of her name in the nations atmosphere; as destructive as the Abomination homonym created from President Obama's name and position. These two high profile public figures support this scripture.*(Ephesian 6:12)... wrestling against Spiritual wickedness in high places.* You cannot get much higher than a President in a Nation in the physical world.

Although Bible scholars has said this scripture is referring to the Devil; the name interpretation of "Degeneres-degenerate" and "Obama Nation-*Abomination*" can create a powerful summoning Spirit for the Devil every time they are spoken or thought of.

Jerry Falwell, the leader of the Moral Majority; did pick up on how appropriate her name was to her sexual orientation. In an interview, he refer to her as "Ellen Degenerate" instead of her birth name "Degeneres". Falwell had no idea how much truth was in that pronunciation. He was using a play on words...based on her Gay confession.

While on the topic of her profession as a talk show host, I like to point out a common observation of publicized Homosexuals.

It amazes me, when a Homosexual is being discuss, how their sexual orientation overshadow everything else. For example, "yes he or she is great at their job...he/she is Gay you know". And any other profession..."isn't he or she gay"? She is Bisexual...but she is good. If you are a working on a public job, when you are introduce...when walking away from you, it is whispered, he/she is gay, queer, faggot, ferry, homosexual, bisexual, transgender, or some form of gesture is indicated, to let one know your abnormal sexual orientation.

You are not known for your talent or your profession you work so hard for, instead, you are known for your sexual orientation. These responses are mostly of a negative nature. Believe it or not, it looses you business. Another reason why this should be a private and personal matter...for the sake of your "lively hood".

Homosexuality makes people uncomfortable. Why? Because its ungodly and the average persons instincts knows this behavior is against the laws of God and nature. So the question is: Do you want to be recognize for your talent or your sexual orientation? A heterosexual for the most part, is not dominated by their sexual orientation. Except on the occasion, when one sex surpasses doing something that is notoriously done by the opposite sex. This is what is happening to Ellen Degeneres. Being Gay supersede her profession. It is strange that she is a comedian. Based on what you have read so far, do you think Homosexuality is funny or a laughing matter?

Another observation on Ellen Degeneres, is that, the pronunciation of the name Degeneres can give an English instructor some trouble. By sound it could be almost a homonym and by spelling and interpretation...almost a synonym. Nevertheless, by interpreting her name, one will see how her name relates to the Bible on Same Sex Relationships.

By taking her name "Ellen" and add an "H" at beginning like this; "Hellen", and then adding a "d" at the end like this; "Hellend", we come up with two complete words..."Hell end". Actually, when the whole name Ellen Degeneres is spoken; the "d" in the phrase "Hell end" comes from her last name..."degeneres"..."Hell en_degeneres". By pronunciation, her whole name create the phrase "Hell end Degenerates." Her complete name, when called, is dictating the fate of her loyal followers as well. This is proof of the "s" at the end of her birth name. Her birth name Degeneres ends with "s"...the English language denotes this to mean more than one. Also, prove she was born to be leader of the Pack. When you embrace someone, you embrace their name first; with all the good and bad that goes with it.

To be "first" is also found within her name Degeneres as well.

In her name De*gene*res, you have the word *"Genesis"* (De-**Gene**-re-**s**) almost spelled out. Of which, *"Genesis"*, by definition, means first. So being "first" in something; had programmed her all her life...leading to her being first to confess being Gay on a public stage.

By her being first, she brings a lot things to surface about female homosexuality. I concluded in my personal observation that lesbianism has something to do with the fathers. Fathers desiring a boy can creates a "Butch" type of girl. Like women desiring a Girl can create a Gay man. This just support the fact that parents does have something to do with their Gay children.

But the very Beautiful woman I mention earlier, that gives themselves to another woman, is something that takes place after the girl is born. These are "Daddy Girls". Fathers that have daughters that are beautiful and she become a lesbian has gotten too much energy from fathers' love. Some times fathers, with his love to his daughter can give a lot of masculine energy in his love. If you doesn't want your beautiful daughter to be in this life choice; there is not but one thing to do to stop this. Let her know, "YOU ARE DONE WITH HER"...and Mean it!!! If you are feeding her too much masculine energy as love, this stops it. Take it from me; she will feel the lost of her Daddy's love and...will get on natures course. There are certain types of love some people can't live without. This is not a theory...this is from experience. I also witness, a beautiful Daddy's girl; where Dad gave in...which I believe, contribute to his early death.

With Ellen Degeneres, her Daddy's Girl love, is locked in. Her first named is very similar to her daddy's name. Look at the similarity of her father's name Elliot Degeneres to her name Ellen Degeneres. Whether her Daddy support her are not; it want affect her. Because of the dominating matching letters "Ell" in Elliot and Ellen. And she fulfills the family sound name...Degeneres-Degenerate. This means that the only way she could fulfill the destiny of "Degeneres-degenerate" family name, is to be female... living a male role. That is why I mention that she was fulfilling one of her destinies.

If you look closer, you can see another word formulating in "Degeneres"; the word *"generation"*...De-*gener*-es. I take this to be the length of time, the publicity of this behavior to last in America after her confession...I mean..."coming out of the closet." That was April 1996. So you can start the count down from there. The question now is, what scale will the number of years a generation be based on. By being the first, she set the length of time in her name, of how long the publicity of homosexuality be a nuisance in our nation.

Note: I like to point out, that with the interpretation of Ellen, this is not saying all women named "Ellen" or even "Helen" have this interpretation. Throughout the above mention book, *"The Half Have Never Been Told"*; it shows that the last name is what generates the interpretation of the first name and vice verse. In Ellen Degeneres case, the last name determines the interpretation of the first name.

Also, in the above reference book, it will explain why the letter "H" was used. It goes on to explains how the "H" was formed and its duty in word creation. But the use of the "H" in this case is for gender identity. Whether she consider herself female with "H" from Her...or whether she is the male of her dyke marriage...with "H" from He. Regardless, the name "ellen" cries out for "H"...Hell.

Earlier, I mention OT law is about the physical and NT scriptures is about the spiritual. Ellen Degeneres name interpretation is the Spiritual (NT) of Sodom and Gomorrah (OT).

The earthly destruction of Sodom and Gomorrah symbolizes the Spiritual punishment of those who practice the Homosexual behavior. Read what the NT has to say in the book of *Jude (1:7)*; *Even as Sodom and Gomorrah and the cities about them in like manner, giving themselves over to fornication, and going after strange flesh, are set forth for an example, suffering the **vengeance of eternal fire.** In* other words, *"Hell end Degenerates".*

I have syllabicated Ellen Degeneres name, to show how it affects the atmosphere, and give the Sodom and Gomorrah affect on her loyal followers. So now, let's look at how the interpretation of Sodom and Gomorrah has a message much more powerful than her name.

By interpreting Sodom and Gomorrah, this is what you get when syllabicating "So-dom" like this: "So doom.". When I dissect the name Go-mor-r-ah as such, I get the phrase *"**Go mor**als **r**ight Jehov**ah**"*.

This is how we get that phrase..."Go" remain as is, "mor" prefix for "morals", the second "r" stand for "right" and "ah" coming at the end of Gomorrah, parallels with the "ah" coming at the end of Jehovah. (*Jehovah is another name that refer to God in the OT*).

When you pronounce Sodom and Gomorrah together, this is the interpretation: *"So doom...Go morals...right Jehovah".* "Jehovah right(ed) or corrected the morals of the two cities by sending out the righteous and destroying the wicked".

The name "Gomorrah" also has the time of the destruction once the Angels arrived. "Gomorrah" syllabicate into Go-morr-ah ...interprets as "*Go* to*morr*ow Jehov*ah*". As the story went in the Bible, Sodom and Gomorrah were destroyed(*So doom*ed) the next day(*Go* to*morr*ow) by the angels(Jehov*ah*).

Note: The subconscious has the power to interpreted many differ message from one pronunciation of a name-word all at the same time.

The "So doom" interpretation-definition mean "at great extent". In our day, the English Language definition of "Go tomorrow" could be "any day".

This little demonstration, is to show how consistent the interpretation of Sodom and Gomorrah are, when comparing the Biblical historical information of the event. Also, to let you know, how much action a word/name spoken over a period time can create.

These interpretation of the two cities, can even suggest their behavior was shaped by the names of the cities. Also, Based on the *Leviticus 20:13* scripture, with the phrase; *"surely be put to death"* indicate a Homosexual is *"So Doom"*.

Sodom and Gomorrah interpretation in our society of today; in the English Language, would have drawn Homosexuals to those two cities. We can support that theory with one of our own States of mass Homosexuality...California.

California is the largest populated state in the Nation and the largest state of Homosexuality and Same Sex Marriage because of that. Not to mention, the state that is the driving force behind promoting Same Sex marriage nationwide through Hollywood. This little interpretation demonstration will show you why.

When you syllabicate Ca-li-fornia as such, "Ca"" is prefix for "Can"..."li" is prefix for "live" and "fornia" is prefix and contraction for "fornicator/fornication". Means that, when California is spoken or pronounced, it produces the phrase in the atmosphere: *"Can live fornicators/fornication"*. On the other hand, if you syllabicate Ca-lif_fornia this way "lif" is prefix for "life or lift". This interpretation is *"Can lift the life of fornication."*

Jokes are made about California as *"Californication"* all the time, and people doesn't realize the reality of those type of comments. Not realizing, that California is named for illicit sex behavior...like Sodom and Gomorrah.

Whereas, the first interpretation draws all kind of illicit sex acts...with Same Sex Marriage being the worst; the second interpretation with the word *lift*, is saying, that this state *lift* or promote all sort of illicit sex acts. All these interpretation are happening simultaneously when California is pronounced.

As you can see, from this interpretation of California, it is similar to "So doom" from "Sodom"...drawing acts of destruction. This just prove as stated above, that if Sodom and Gomorrah were the names of two cities in America today, the above English Language interpretation would have drawn people that were "Doomed". For clarity, it is saying, because of the people described in "Sodom and Gomorrah"....Homosexuals are "Doomed."

These interpretation illustrate, how differ names in differ times has the same meaning, and a high percentage of the same results. The interpretation process show how words breaks downs in your "mind/soul" on a mass scale...when publicize continually in the Atmosphere.

Imagine taking a pill. The pill dissolve within you to perform its intended task. Interpretation, let you see how word break down within you the same way. This is why I interpret certain words and names to drive a point home. Jesus used this analogy of word break down in *planting seeds on good ground.(Mark 4:8).*

The secret behind this type of interpretation process; is to let you know, what can happen if enough people think on a certain issue. And enough people thinking negative about Homosexuality, or the right people thinking negative about it; can bring destruction like that of Sodom and Gomorrah.

This brings me to another big mystery I must share about the interpretation process. God has design it, so we can be our best friend or our own worse enemy. He has design us to "self predict" our own destiny as well as our own "self destruction"...personally and collectively. These differences are determine by what you focus on in word-thoughts. Or...what is being dominated in the public through the media. The application of this interpretation process illustrates, how words and names has within them to make things happen in a desire or designed way. These interpretation are presented, to let you know, the affects of certain names or words when greatly publicized.

By understanding this, is what make *John 1:1* one of...if not... the most powerful scriptures in the Bible: *In beginning was the word, and the word was with God and the word was God.*

The definition of the term "God" is defined as the Supreme Being or Ultimate Ruler. The words we think or focus on...with their definition and what they represent, is what control our destiny and fate. Those words are our "God"(Supreme in our Being and ultimate Ruler) the Apostle John was writing about in *John 1:1.*

I am trying to make this point crystal clear; (whether its a family or nation)....God's word is final. If a particular action in

OT Bible carries a particular penalty and the NT Scriptures are consistent with it, you can believe it's going to happen.

Its hard NOT to think on negative consequence of Same Sex Relationships when the media is shoving it down our throats 24/7 to a quietly unreceptive nation. The good news is; the more they promote, the sooner it will be over.

As mention above; things from the Bible may have a differ name, but can have the same interpretation in results. Like Sodom and Gomorrah verses modern day California.

Here is another example, we have a Father of our country name Abraham (President Lincoln)as the Bible describe the Patriot Father Abraham. The Bible Patriot Abraham was given a revelation by God that his descendents would be in Slavery for 400 years(*Genesis 15:13*). And America President Abraham freed a people from slavery, eventually, the same length of time.

Also, Bible Abraham tried to intercede on behalf of Sodom and Gomorrah's destruction. He started bargaining with the Angels on their behalf with the question: *"if fifty righteous was found would he spare Sodom and Gomorrah(genesis 18:26)*. Comparably, America is composed of *fifty* states.

That fifty righteous, Father Abraham mention above, could be for America of today. (*When making an association like this, I call this reading between the lines of the Bible in relation to America*). Refer back to the *Leviticus 20:13* law against Same Sex relationship and how I compare that numerical scripture(20:13) to the big push for Same Sex Couples in America; in the year 2013.

Let's go back to Abraham bargaining with the Angels to spare Sodom and Gomorrah. Because the Angel agreed so easily, Bible Abraham pressed the Angels to spare the two cities by decreasing the number of righteous people until he got down to ten righteous. *Genesis 18:32*, (Abraham is speaking to the Angels)

And he said, Oh let not the Lord be angry, and I will speak yet but this once; Peradventure ten shall be found there(righteous people). *And he said, I will not destroy it for ten's sake.* Abraham was satisfied with the number ten because he knew that this would include his nephew Lot's whole family who lived in Sodom and Gomorrah. And after this the Angels left.

The Bible is very consistent through both Old and New Testaments in confirming that homosexuality is sin. Here is a list of Scriptures from Old and New Testament that proves that:(*Genesis 19:1-13, Leviticus 18:22 &20:13, Romans1:26-27, 1Corinthian 6:9 Jude 1:7*).

On the Homosexual issue, the NT scriptures reinforces what the OT Law had declared since the Law was given to Moses *(Leviticus 20:13)*. The difference between the OT and NT is that the NT offers hope and restoration to those caught up in the sin of homosexuality through the redeeming power of Jesus.

Not only is God consistent with OT Law and NT Scripture on issues such as Same Sex Relationship. God is consistent in America on "All" issues supported by OT Law and NT Scriptures.

For example, it was mention earlier, how the Israelite were in slavery for 400 years and the Negro Slave in America was equally in slavery for 400 years. God sent a deliverer for Israelite call Moses. In America, God sent a deliverer for the Negro slave call President Abraham Lincoln. God gave the deliverer for the Negro Slaves in America an OT powerful name...Abraham...to go alone with the OT act of freeing slaves like Moses.

With that being said. Doesn't it stand to reason, because of the destruction of Sodom and Gomorrah's on a massive group of people praticing Same Sex Relationship; that this nation will receive an equal consequent by legalizing Same Sex marriage nationwide? If God is consistent with America on one issue from the Bible, he will be consistent on another.

The example above, of the Twin Towers destroyed on 911 being symbolic of Sodom and Gomorrah: took place, when Same Sex Relationship was not legal in America. Do you think, God is going to honor The Supreme Court legalization of Same Sex Marriage and override the laws of Moses and the NT Apostles warnings against this behavior? As the destruction of Sodom and Gomorrah was by fire and brimstone from Heaven; there will be a like in the after life.

Whereas, President Obama name creates the homonym *"Abomination"* from the OT of the Bible....Ellen Degeneres name interprets into a Synonym phrase...*"Hell end degenerates"* from the NT of the Bible. Although, these two names are highly publicize, making for strong advocates of today's Same Sex relationship problem in our country...*they are "NOT"...the origin of the nation's problem on other evils such as this.*

The origin of the problems of massive "Out of control" Evils in our country today can be traced back to our Founding Fathers. It started with the type of Government they chose as a *Democracy*. This Government would not be like Great Britain King arbitrary Despotism that the thirteen colonies won their freedom from. This Government would put the power in the hands of the people... *Government of the people, by the people, and for the people.*

The process in which this Government would be executed, would be called the *"Democratic Process"*. Each person in this Democracy, exercising their rights through the Democratic process would be call a *Democrat*. But little did our Founding Fathers realize from the word *Democracy, Democratic* and *Democrat;* that the first four letters of each of those words are four fifths of the word *"Demon"*.

Using the word that reflects each American's individuality...."Democrat"; by thesaurus pronunciation, is syllabicated like this: *Dem-o-crat*...with three syllables. But when the average person pronounces it; it is syllabicated like this:

Demo-crat...two syllables. With that syllabication; "Demo" is lacking one letter("n") of the word *"Demon"*. The remaining part "crat" is also lacking one letter..."e" in two places...forming the word *"create"*. Meaning, that every time the word "Democrat" is spoken, written, or thought; it promotes the atmosphere *"Demon Create"*. This means that speaking the name *"Democrat"*; acts...as a summoning power for evil..."*Demon Create*".

One can conclude, that *"The Devil"* has been hiding in "Plain Sight" in America for more than 230 years. And we constantly is feeding it to do more Evil...like the Publicity of Homosexuality... being pushed by the media. The "media" is being driven by this *"Demon Create"*-Democratic atmosphere in our nation.

Being an individual call Democrat(*Demon Create*), is the word that drew the name Obama, into our government atmosphere... creating todays *Obama nation-Abomination*; long before he was born or thought of.

Note: So Mr. President(Obama), of the Democrat Party; being called a *Demon*, is not really that far of a stretch after all. It is not really a big laughing joke as you think it is.

The Political Party Democrat, suppose to represent the epitome of our style of Government; and yet, this Political Party, is responsible for every major evil that has been in our country.

We mention earlier, of Andrew Jackson, the first President of our modern day Democrat Party. Which is the party that promoted slavery. This is also the Party that fought "TO KEEP" Slavery during the Civil War. Slavery has been our longest lasting public evil in our nation so far.

With the Party name: "Democrat-*Demon Create*," you can understand why African-Americans still cannot get pass Slavery. In the last election 93 percent of African-American voted this party. Their party affiliation of Democrat is not something force upon them like slavery, this is their choice. And yet, the African-Americans complains all the time of the evil of this system. When this is not even the party that gave them their freedom. Which means, that the evil in modern day America that is brought upon African-Americans are of their own making. Because...African Americans of today, votes for the party(Democrat) that created the KKK and other White terrorist groups.

I made this point to show how Satan has blinded pretty much the majority of African-Americans in our nation with this *"Demon Create"* atmosphere. I could never understand, why African-Americans as a whole, voted "Democrat" until I interpret *"Demon Create"* from its pronunciation. This just mean, that the "Democrat Slave masters" *(Demon Create)*done a real job on the majority of the Negro Slaves; to affect their modern day descendants...voting the Democratic Party. As oppose to the Republican party that gave their freedom. Some will come to realize why so much evil happens to modern day African-American. *Revelation 2:4 : Nevertheless, I have somewhat against thee, because thou hast left thy first love*...Republican Party whom gave you your freedom.

Now this *"Demon Create"* atmosphere of our Democracy, has blinded a whole nation. Starting with our Strongest Executive part of our Government...the President on the issue of Homosexuality.

And now, the one thing that President Obama(Obama Nation...*Abomination)* and Ellen Degeneres(*Hell end degenerates*) has in common, is this "Democrat-*Demon Create*" Party. This party supported the Evil of Slavery; and now, the evil of Homosexuality by Bible standards. From the *"Demon Create"* interpretation of Democrat; we all have a better understanding of "WHY"...this party is responsible for every major evil in America.

Even Hollywood; indirectly, has understood part of this process of how the interpretation of *"Demon Create,"* from the word *"Democrat,"* is responsible for the evil that is reaping

Havoc on our land through "Homosexuality". I have seen some television episode; in order to summons certain forces; a particular word or name is spoken three times. Think about how many times *"Democrat"* is mention in one day (*Demon Create*)...a lot of summoning power.

This means, that not only did our founding fathers create a Great Government called Democracy: they created all the evils that went with it. This Evil now that is plaguing our nation of Same Sex Relationship has been kept alive throughout the history of this nation because of the word..."Democrat-*Demon Create*". Only the belief of the Bible with preaching and demonstration of the Gospel has kept it under control.

With the ministers of today, obeying man (the Government) rather than God; evil is being manifested in many other ways than just Same Sex Relationship. Just look at your daily News. The bad or Evil take center stage over the Good News. If there is...any good news during that News broadcast.

All this brings me to the question; of why would our Founding Fathers be led unknowingly to choose this form of Government.... Democracy: with an interpretation of *"Demon Create"*?

The answer that I received from that question, was very interesting: and that was, they unknowingly, brought this on themselves. The moment the thirteen colonies White men began to copulate with the Negro Slave women; they became part of the "Canaan curse of Servitude". You see...the Negro Slave woman was the "forbidden fruit".

After children started to be born from the Slave masters raping the Negro Slave woman; Great Britain's King George III, Politically, started treating the slave masters the way they treated the Negro slaves. Just read the list of complains drew up by the thirteen colonies against King George III in the *"The Declaration of Independence"*. King George III dehumanize the thirteen colonies, the way the White Slave masters dehumanize the Negro Slaves.

They *"created"* this *"Demon"(Demon-create)* on a personal level (*Democrat*) when they Raped the slave woman. This is what started the Racial Hatred in Negro Slaves that cause Black Homosexuality. And the Civil War, was the Negro Slaves revenge, that started the Hatred of the White man...making both races,"contributing factor" of the nationwide Homosexuality of today.

It make sense, why we today, as a nation, have the perverseness of Homosexuality; because of the perverseness of the White slave masters raping the Negro Slave women. This also strengthen the belief of the number 13 as "bad luck", associated in the numerical make up of Homosexuality; discussed earlier. That goes alone with our original 13 colonies of the nation. This *"Demon Create"* Government is of our own making.

Yes...God was with our founding fathers in obtaining their Independence because he ordained a purpose for this nation. The same as he was with Adam and Eve after they bit of the forbidden fruit. When Eve gave in to Satan; with the Forbidden fruit: that meant the Devil will always be around. And just like the thirteen colonies(now America), that gave into the "forbidden fruit" of raping the Negro Slave woman...through our Democracy; God uniquely kept the Devil around us...*Demon Create*.

After the Slave Masters, unknowingly, took of the "forbidden fruit" of raping the Negro Slave women; he created a couple of forbidden fruits of his own. The White man made the "Black Man" the forbidden fruit of his White women; and later, made "His White Women", the "forbidden fruit of the Black man. Why I conclude the White man created these two "forbidden fruit" is because, the White man was the only one doing the punishment in both these cases.

What was happening here, is that, God uniquely applied Adam and Eve's world, when the White man raped the Negro Slave Women: as the forbidden fruit with *"Demon Create"*. Then, when the White man created his forbidden fruit of the White woman and the Black man; this was the same as Noah cursing his descendant Canaan for the first act of Homosexuality in the second New World. So both world's.... Adam/Eve and Noah's world were created in America the same time....God's world(Adam/Eve) and man's world(Noah). Noah's world is the one we live in today. This is why it is being call in some Religious establishments as "Man's Day".

From all this, God punished the White Man and our nation for the "forbidden Fruit" action of raping the Negro Slave woman from *"before"* our "Nations Birth"...up until now. The same as God did mankind; the moment Eve took of the forbidden fruit in the Garden of Eden, up until now. By referencing the book *"The Half Have Never been Told"*; it discloses the whole "forbidden fruit" of Adam and Eve in the names of our First President and vice President families. This Revelation, is just one of America's Big Handwriting on the Wall. Now you have the Full story of Homosexuality and *"where it really begin"*; from its origin, up to modern day America.

So now let's explore the solution to this *"Demon Create"* society that we have created.

The Problem...the Solution

Homosexuals have painted themselves as victims in our Nation. I hope that from the information I have presented in this book, thus far, have proved that they are "Not" the victim, but the perpetrators. Basing that on *Leviticus 20:13* and the nation's moral foundation started by our Founding Fathers.

A House Divided against itself will not stand(Mark 3:25). Jesus spoke those words to skeptics when they were questioning his method of healing. Abraham Lincoln took this scripture as a title to a speech regarding the increasingly growing controversy over the Slave issue prior to becoming President.

He used this scripture to stir up the minds of people on the issue of Slavery. In detailing that scripture, he confirm that this nation could not remain half slave and half free. And now using Lincoln's motivation for that title speech, I will echo this Bible verse a second time on the issue of the legalization of Same Sex Marriage in the nation.

This nation can not remain "Half Homosexual and Half Heterosexual. The Homosexual issue in our nation is never going to end until it is handle fairly and properly. Religious believers values are being hampered with, because of the legalization of Same Sex Marriage in our nation...as we have constantly protested throughout this book.

This nation is "quietly" divided because of this issue. It is hard for me to believe, that our Nation leaders cannot see that this issue...Same Sex Relationships, violates every Religion that uses the Holy Bible: especially, the King James version. Throughout the Bible...it declares this behavior ungodly, and not excepted in the "true believers" place of Worship. In return, violating millions of Americans first Constitutional Amendment right.

The reason it violates people religious rights, is because, it is described in OT Law and NT Scripture, that Same Sex Relationships, goes against God's natural order of procreation. Also, it is described as a *disgusting* sin by definition. The actual word that is used in OT Law is *"Abomination"*. Throughout this book, we have given many ways it is an evil that violates the sanctity of marriage. The most publicized sign that this is an evil, is the way it was handle in the Supreme court; when legalizing Same Sex Marriage.

I believe that a modern day Abraham Lincoln would have suggested, that the best way to settled this issue of Same Sex Marriage; is through the Democratic Process...Government of the People...by the People...for the People(The Gettysburg Address).

Concerning the issue of Slavery, on how to save the Union in President Lincolns day; he made these quotes: "if he could save the union without freeing the slaves he would do that, and if I could save it by freeing all the slaves I would do it; and if I could save it by freeing some and leaving others alone I would also do that." Lincoln...unlike many Presidents upon entering the White House, had a clear mandate..."Save the Union".

Applying that same rationale Lincoln used in Saving the union; I think that he would have suggested another worth while Democratic process on settling the Same Sex Marriage issue of today. This very practical and worth while process is used by all groups on major decisions..."The Majority Rule".

"The Same Sex Marriage and publicity of this life style should have been(should be) decided at the voting Booth. This is the only fair solution, because of the number of religious denomination that Same Sex Marriage violates.

The decision to legalize Same Sex Marriage goes against God's rationale in the creation of Man and Woman. Therefore, every voting age Adult should have a say in what the future of their children should be expose to. After all, Same Sex Couples cannot produce a future of children. We have demonstrated what kind of future we can expect if a world is over run by Same Sex Marriages.

By settling this issue at the voting booth; by the majority rule method...whether the voter turn out is a "million" more on either side or a lesser number: the issue would be closed. That is the definition of Democracy...Government of the People...By the People and For the people. That is what a modern day President Abraham Lincoln would have done. If not this, he would have done something very wise, unique and even shocking to settle this issue.

While I am on the subject of President Lincoln; I like to say, every twentieth century and twentieth first century President would like to be as Great as President Lincoln: but they can't. Modern day Presidents doesn't understand the depth of Lincolns' Religious conviction that guided his actions. Lincoln didn't even know the depth of his religious conviction until he was chosen to be President.

His Religious conviction was anchored...first by being named after one of the world's greatest Religious Patriot...Abraham. This "name", through the attempted sacrifice of his son Isaac, set the world on course for the Coming Messiah. Of which, President Abraham Lincoln, had to actually, sacrifice, through death, one of his sons while being President. And secondly, reading the Bible over and over as a youngster, put him on a path similar to that of

111

Bible Patriots and Apostles. In other words, he would have known how to handle the Homosexual issue; without all the Post drama brought on by the Supreme Court five-four ruling.

By the Bible being the most common book to read in Lincoln's day; he read it with passion. And because of the Spiritual impact of the name Abraham; what he read from the Bible, stuck and shaped him into Lincoln the President. And after being President, the Bible supported his Emancipation Proclamation; ending slavery and eventually, segregation. Modern technology, would have help him make the decision of settling this issue of Same Sex Marriage at the voting booth. In return; would set a more positive tone on this issue World Wide.

We have mention, the five-four ruling of the American Supreme Court declaring DOMA unconstitutional several times... leading to the legalizing of Same Sex Marriage. But we need to dig deeper on those Supreme Court Judges that voted in favor of Same Sex Marriages.

The first big problem of the Supreme Court Ruling on this issue, is that, the judges were not schooled in Bible OT Law. They were schooled in American Law. And the most important information on this issue, whether modern day or Bible days, is in OT Law and NT Scriptures. To qualify for a Supreme Court Judge in America, one had to have great insight on laws of the land and the Constitution; not of Bible OT Law.

It "IS NOT" mandatory to have a Religious background to become a Supreme Court Judge. That is because, Religious beliefs are a choice. However, on the issue of Same Sex Marriage...a religious background by all Supreme Court Judges would have rendered a more Godly and conservative verdict on this controversial issue. This is because, most American's Religion teaches, that God, the Supreme Ruler, is mankind's, final Judge. This parallels with our "Supreme Court" rendering not only the final and ultimate verdict on National issues; but supposedly, the best verdict for its people.

Modifying a phrase from a quote from the TV series "ARROW"; I have this to say to the Supreme Court decision declaring DOMA unconstitutional..."**SUPREME COURT JUDGES OF AMERICA; YOU HAVE FAILED THIS NATION!**" In this ruling, the Supreme Court missed the mark on this verdict. Because...there is too much post "DOMA Unconstitutional" drama.

Another problem of the Supreme Court Ruling in favor of Same Sex marriage, the media did not exploit the gender bias on this controversial issue. Three of the five Judges declaring DOMA unconstitutional were woman. Is this an issue? Yes it is an issue when it comes to Homosexuality. Let's explore how.

These three woman were not interpreting the issue of Same Sex Marriage as "unbiased Judges of the Law": they where interpreting this issue as "bias mothers". If the panel of Supreme Court Judges would have been all men; DOMA would have been declared Constitutional. This is not male chauvinist... this is fact.

Starting from the Bible days, God has always used men for creating and interpreting the Law. There is no where in the Bible, a woman was used to established a Law for the future of mankind. Except for the Book of Esther. She being Queen, she had the kings permission to sign his name and use his ring to create any law needed for her people(*Esther 8:8*). She still had to get permission from the King...her husband, as Eve's curse went.

I am not saying that a woman is not cable of being a great Supreme Court Judge. On many issues of national interest, a female perspective is greatly needed. The fact is: a women can not be unbiased on certain issue because its too close to their God-given nature.

A woman's role starting from the expulsion from the Garden of Eden was spelled out with clarity. That very role given then, affected the outcome of this Same Sex Issue of today. Which was the wrong outcome.

We all know the Garden of Eden story of what went on; who received what punishments God dealt out for all involved in the *"biting of the forbidden fruit"* incident.

The woman's punishment was to bear children...in pain. The average woman instinct is to protect their child. Her love to her children is suppose to be unconditional. By childbearing being describe in the Bible as the very first responsibility after the forbidden fruit incidence; this becomes part of her nature. This nature is rooted in both subconscious and conscience mind of good mothers. Meaning, it can control good mothers on issue like Homosexuality without her being aware.

These three female Supreme court Judges, without a doubt, thought they were being fair on this issue. But actually, unknowingly, were being very bias in this ruling. When God told Bible Abraham to sacrifice his Son Isaac as an Obedient test... what would have happen if Abraham would have shared this information with Sarah his wife?

Keep in mind, one of the main arguments that were used to render the five four ruling of DOMA Unconstitutional, was about the children of Same Sex Parents. It was said, that children of Same Sex parents will be less valued than male and female parents. Of course they would...for good reason at that. The Bible says Same Sex couples are an *"Abomination"(Leviticus 18:22 &20:13)*. The reason that the argument came up of Same Sex couples being "less value" than the God ordain family of man and woman, **"BECAUSE...THEY "ARE" LESS VALUE"!!!** What do you think **"ABOMINATION"** mean?

We established earlier, that Same Sex Couples has no right raising children to begin with. The CHOICE of their UNGODLY lifestyle as a Same Sex couple suggested that they cared nothing for Procreation.

IF just...ONE.....of the "female" Supreme Court Judges would have declared DOMA Constitutional, I could not make this claim. But all three of these woman...voting the same; suggest that there are certain issue woman cannot be objected on. These three female judges should have "RECUSE" themselves on the issue of legalizing Same Sex Marriage.

Paul the apostle of Jesus Christ had this to say: *1 Timothy 2:12-15....For Adam was first formed, then Eve. And Adam was not deceived, but the woman being deceived was in the transgression. She shall be saved in childbearing...* The Bible also records Paul as saying, it wasn't good for women to speak in the church. Admittedly, in modern day America, that is being Chauvinistic. I view that as going a little too far. But let's look at the merits of Paul's thinking.

The above scripture is indicating that the woman is more susceptible to the notion of evil than the man...on certain issues. By now, you should know; that the evil of Homosexuality is one of those issues. Therefor, Paul's recommendation above is correct. The above scripture, also pointed out, her natural duty in relation to her child. That seals the idea of "RECUSE".

The woman was deceive by the Devil and convince Adam(two male Supreme Court Judges). Regardless of how foolish this may sound. Each one of the Female Supreme Judges is symbolic a letter that spell the name E-v-e. Eve is three letters and the two men that went alone with this decision are symbolic of the two A's in Adam. Referring to Eve, persuading Adam to join her in eating the forbidden fruit, is like the three women persuading the two men judges on this issue. To you that think that this is ridiculous; this is what Jesus would call *"the jot and tittle"* on the issue of Same Sex Marriage.(*Matt:5:18*)

The point of this is not that woman are not fit for the Supreme Court, again, this was not an issue for the Supreme Court..."PERIOD"!!! It certainly is not the decision of nine people that comes down to "one vote". This one vote, I remind you... affects the very foundation of human existence in America... and the World. If that one vote was God, that would have been something different.

It should be no surprise, that those three female judges were nominated by our last two elected Democrat Presidents. Keep in mind, our above interpretation of *"Demon Create"* from the name "Democrat". This is another example, of how the evil generated from Democrat, is affecting our nation. Two of the females judges were nominated by President Obama. Of which these two judges, were the deciding factor of DOMA being declared unconstitutional.

In the outset of this book, I stated that, there are certain truths we are going to have to accept before we can come to a fair solution to this Same Sex problem in our nation. The three female Supreme Court Judges ruling in favor of Same Sex Marriage are one of them. And to add to that; many racist believe a Black President would bring our Nation down. And because of the many ways President Obama has supported the issue of Same Sex marriage... those type of statements are becoming a reality.

The legalization of Same Sex Marriage affects two majors minority fights throughout the history of our Nation. The Black Man and women rights in highly influential roles of present and future Government.

In years to come, when people understand the pivotal role those three female judges played, in unleashing this evil of Same Sex Marriage on our nation...could have adverse affect on women nomination as Supreme Court Judges. With the fact, that a woman cannot be unbiased on issues pertaining to Children. Being a mother, overshadows her judgment of interpreting the law in an unbiased capacity.

Throughout this book, I have described Same Sex Relationship as an evil born out of a darkness. I discovered that a T.V. Series like "Supernatural" does a very good job of promoting extreme evil as darkness. When a program like this has eleven successful seasons, it gets my attention. I have to believe, the producers are doing something right. So I went back and watch all eleven seasons.

Though much of the series may be fictitious in many episodes; there is a lot of truth in the series. The producer, keeping up with modern day, added a Gay character. She is portrayed as one of the good guys. But even the person that played that role was killed off viciously in the end. That characters death, was in line with the Bible's penalty on Same Sex Relationship.(*Leviticus 20:13*) This let me know, that the producers of this program, are keeping with the Bible Scripture guide lines; whether they are aware of this, or not.

One of the things I know they got right for those series is the title..."Supernatural". There is no place on earth the word "Supernatural" is use more than in the Church or a Religious setting. I have given irrefutable prove, that Same Sex Relationships is a Church and Religious issue.

To the religious people, if you haven't notice, that each sin that is committed, is based on a certain level of darkness. The punishment in OT law usually suggest that as well. The sins of the OT born out of the greatest darkness is punishable by Death.

You wouldn't kill a person for what one call a "little white lie". But if it is a lie that can cause death on an innocent; then it comes from a very dark place; modern day court refer to as perjury... punishable by imprisonment. If any sin in OT law is punishable by death, as mention earlier, this means it brings harm to others:

and...a detriment to mankind. By now you should understand "why and how" Homosexuality is the second worst sin-crime in the world: the first of course, is murder.

On the other hand, NT scriptures are against all sin...small or great. Because, small sins grow into larger sin. Jesus gave this example about *committing adultery starting as lust in the heart (Matt.5:27&28). He said if you have lusted you have already sin.*

The television is exploiting this darkness of evil that's reaping havoc on our nation in many difference ways. So I am going to take this darkness to another level and go back to its origin.

I am getting ready to move into a very controversial area with this darkness.

It was stated earlier, that the Homosexual community equated Same Sex Couples as the same as an interracial couple. Some television series try to promote this as well.

In many T.V. Series, I have noticed, if there is an interracial couple in a series, they push a Gay couple. Then Gays, feel like when they meet a Black person in society; they have a supporter for their cause. Contrary to what some may think; African Americans are not all monolithic in their thinking.

Nevertheless, what I am getting ready to tell you is why Gays feel like there is a connection between their life choice and Black people. This revelation is not "conscience" to a Gay: it is an unconscious or subconscious Spiritual manifestation.

Once the servitude curse was spoken by Noah; the darkness that causes Homosexuality within; started to move outward of man...physically. Earlier, I mention, it took about a hundred years for Noah to rid himself of this Garden of Eden *original darkness...* the darkness that enter the first couple Adam and Eve. But what we didn't tell you was, each phase of this darkness...as it surface to the outside of man's flesh...created a race of people. This started after the flood, following the curse of Servitude spoken to Canaan by his grand father Noah.

The finale phase of this darkness, as it made its way out of man, took man back to the original place it entered. Historians has traced the Garden of Eden to Africa. That goes alone with the belief that criminal returns to the scene of the crime. The biting of the forbidden fruit, was definite a crime.

With that in mind, many Black people believe that the first man was Black because of the Garden of Eden birthplace; said to be in Africa. I am sorry to disappoint you. Black people was first discovered in Africa, because the instinct of this darkness that first entered man made a full circle. *Isaiah 46:10* saw it this way; *Declaring the end from the beginning, and from ancient times....*

As the last phase of this darkness manifested itself, it change the total color and features of the original man and woman it entered. To be crystal clear on this, I am saying, the original darkness that entered Adam and Eve after Satan deception; created the African dark skinned people.

This darkness in the second New World had the same punishment as the first punishment of Adam...*to work by the sweat of his brow.(Genesis 3:19)*. However, in the case of the first darken sin after Noah Flood; Ham's descendant; starting with Canaan, would be curse to Servitude. Both curses has the same punishment(*Genesis 3:19*). But because of the severity and disgust of the Homosexual sin; a "group of people" would have to work under duress, for an indefinite time to shed the evil of the Homosexual sin- darkness.

As a nation of people were born from this curse; another nation was born to end it. This nation became known as the United States of America. Black people can be considered as the descendants of Canaan. And the final end of the Servitude curse.

Also, if you can wrap your head around the fact, that the final race of people created from the original darkness of the forbidden fruit where Africans; then you understand why; the "original" African woman being raped by the White man during slavery; became the forbidden fruit of America. The original Africans that were brought to America; their "real and true Black skin", was a result of the first and the original darkness, that enter man after the forbidden fruit was eaten. Because...wait for it...the "White man was the first race on earth". Black people probably didn't want to hear that; that is why God chose a Black man to write it.

The original African woman, raped by the White man, is the White man actually entering inside the Darkness of the original sin all over again. It stands to reason, that the White man was the first Race. Because, all other Races of the world, believe the White man is the perpetrated behind all the Evil that exist on earth today.

Furthermore, if you would compare, the original African brought to American skin color; to the "average" African-American of today; you would conclude, we are merely a symbol of the original African. In other words, we are just a representative of who we used to be.

According to the story in Genesis, a fruit was bit that caused the darkness to enter man. Bible translator and interpreters believe it to be the Apple...a red apple at that. But when the original darkness made its way to the outside of man; there was a fruit to keep this darkness on the out side as well. This fruit (not Biblical mention) was called the Watermelon. The red pulp representing the blood of Jesus: the water to wash the sins away. The watermelon was first discovered in Africa. This is why Black people use to be associated with watermelons; by the process for which it was design: to keep the darkness on the outside.

When the Africans were tricked and bought to America and made into slaves; the picking of the cotton while viewing it with the window to the soul...their eyes; made their soul or internals pure...white. When the whiteness (representing purity) within the Negro slave became greater than the external Whiteness of the Slave master; God send a deliverer. (Remember the interpretation of Negro done earlier, as "Need Growth" or "Need to Grow").

Let's make something very clear, about the servitude curse Noah placed on his gran son Canaan resulting from the first act of Homosexuality. When God told Abraham his descendants would be in bondage for four hundred years; God was creating a people that would serve him. When a generation of Israelite were born, that believe that God would send a Savior to deliver them; God send Moses. This is the same purpose for the Negro Slave in America. To be the group of people upholding the religious banner of God; for the nation.

Although the African-American is dark outside; they suppose to be White inside, because of the picking of White cotton in the days of Slavery; preceded by the watermelon eaten in their native land...Africa. When they were freed, they suppose to have maintain this whiteness created from picking cotton; by applying the word of God in their life with the Bible.

But because of the African-American external darkness; the Homosexual community, think Black Americans has a connection to them. Meaning, the darkness in the heart of a born Homosexual(not turned) that causes his condition; mirrors the exterior darkness of an African-American. This is all subconscious to Homosexual; his conscious mind is unaware of this sublime process in action started thousands of years ago. The average Homosexual will never grasp this, because, this process is totally Spiritual.

However, a Black Heterosexual that doesn't support a Homosexual has rid himself of this type of internal darkness. The different is, African-Americans darkness is on the outside, the Homosexual is dealing with that original darkness on the inside: in the heart where everything originate(*Proverbs 4:23*). Because of this original darkness on the inside; is another reason, Homosexuality should not be a pubic issue. God help a Black Homosexual: they have the darkness both in...and outside.

This journey, of the original darkness, I just took you on, from the inside of man to the outside of man, is the reason that God Judges the Heart. *He doesn't judge the outward appearance as man does.1Sam.16:7.* All men are created equally: on the inside. Whether Black is Beautiful or White think they are Superior: it is a personal opinion. That also goes for all other races concerning superiority.

One thing for certain, with God being the judge, all races have the same chances within. This is what confuses the KKK and other Caucasian hate groups against African-American and other minorities. They are looking at the outward appearance.

This darkness that is causing Homosexuality in America, is the original darkness..."the *Cain killing his brother Abel* darkness."

The original sin that entered Eve included deception. And one of the biggest characteristics of deception is confusion. The way Satan confused Eve is with this phrase, *"you want surely die"* (*Genesis 3:4*). Deception involves half truths in order to manipulate a person to a desired end.

This deception is the confusion that Satan has put in a born Homosexual. This same form of deception is used by Gays to *"Turn"* heterosexuals to Gays. The difference in Gays of today with the original sin, is that, it ends a family lineage. The original sin in Adam and Eve started the lineage of descendants.

This darkness from within to the outside, has a modern day consequence in our Political history as well. Andrew Jackson being the first President of today's Democrat Party pushed Slavery. This is also the party that fought to keep slavery in the days of the Civil War. This means, that the darkness "within" that cause Slavery has now surface, symbolically, through President Obama.

Obama being a mix child, symbolize the "complete" process of the darkness traveling from within man to the outside of man. Black father and White mother, means that the darkness once in the white man causing him to act on the evil of Slavery(Democrat President Andrew Jackson) has come to surface in the Democrat party as a Black man...President Obama. Who is now promoting the cause of servitude-slavery... Homosexuality.

If this theory is correct, Obama could possibly be the last Democrat President. And if Homosexuality is dealing with the original darkness; this means that creation has come full circle in America. We are at the end of time. Homosexuality means no procreation...no future.

To add credence to this theory, let's talk about the President who first open the door for public Homosexuals acceptance. This President was Bill Clinton...a Democrat. He was known for eight years as President Bill Clinton. His initials "BC" were not only acronym for his name. The letters *"BC"* are also acronym for *"Before Christ"*. By Bill Clinton being the first American President with the biggest push for public acceptance of Homosexuality. his initials(BC) are saying: *"Before Christ* returns the second time, the Homosexual issue has to be dealt with".

This brings us to the Nations Antidote for Homosexuality. We have already interpret *"Demon Create"* from Democrat, as the cause that made our Nation's Atmosphere conducive for many evil: with the legalization of Same Sex Marriages being the worse. We also concluded, that the Democrat Party is responsible for the evil of both Slavery and Homosexuality. Homosexuality being the crime, and Slavery-Servitude being the punishment.

Another major point that must be reveal, is why it becomes the responsibility of this nation to rid the world of this evil of

Homosexuality. As we revealed, more than once, that this was initiated in the Genesis of America.

When Noah's flood wash away the first world, it created a New World. When Christopher Columbus discovered America, he call it the "New World"; because it was still part of the second world created by Noah's flood. Columbus was at the top of his game when he discovered America. Meaning, from his name interpretation, he became the voice of Jesus Christ.

The water from Noah's flood only receded as the world population grew. The water from Noah's Flood covering America did not recede immediately following the flood. This land was set aside for a special group of people. This group of people were "US"...the United States of America. To get more clarity of this and Christopher Columbus name interpretation reference the book title *"The Half Have Never Been Told"* by *Jolomark Retunah.*

Whereas Bill Clinton is acronym for *"Before Christ"*; Christopher Columbus initials "CC" is acronym for *"Christ Coming"*. The land he discovered would prepare a people for the *"Coming Christ"*. To prove this, the first six letters of Christopher is *"Christ"* and first two letters of Columbus is "Co"...prefix for "Come". [("Come" being one of the most popular words used in the English language that begins with "Co")].

Note: *Speaking of CC as acronym for "Christ Coming" on the very day of me writing this, an iconic American has died...Muhammad Ali. I mention this, because Muhammad Ali enter American History as Cassius Clay. His initials "CC" is also a sign of Christ's Coming. Reference the Book "The Half Have Never Been Told" by Jolomark Retunah. This book will tell you who he really was. How he never tap his true "Greatness"("I Am the Greatest"): because he changed his name from Cassius Clay to Muhammad Ali. He did not know that his birth name Cassius Marcellus Clay was a God Given name for a Higher purpose.*

We mention earlier, for the Wright Brothers flight to be a success, it was a necessity for the name Theodore Roosevelt to be at the pinnacle of power.

Because Presidents Obama's name has created an atmosphere that "contributes" to a great evil; we need a President name that has prove successful for a good-positive atmosphere; in order to counteract this evil. The name that can do this is Theodore...as in President Theodore Roosevelt.

The first four letters of his name *Theo,* are prefix letters for Theocracy. Theocracy is a Government who believes that God is it leader. Theodore Roosevelt being put in power at the origin of the twentieth century, after President McKinley assassination; was a "clear" act of God. Great strides for mankind would be made in the twentieth century...starting with one of the Greatest achievements of mankind...the Airplane.

It was no accident that Theodore Roosevelt face is one of the faces on Mount Rushmore; for being more than just a great President. His name held the key for the salvation of this nation.

Based on the scripture *Isaiah 46:10; God call the end from the beginning...* The twentieth century suppose to ended with the *"Theocratic party-Government";* because, President Theodore Roosevelt was the President that started the twentieth century.

President Roosevelt, after leaving office, felt that there was more for him to do as President. He felt the need for another party; because, as a post President, he came up with the "Bull Moose Progress party". Roosevelt was on track with the new party idea, but did not realize, his "Actual name"(Theodore) held the key for that Party.

There are many clues, that suggest our founding fathers, unknowingly, laid the foundation for a Religious form of Government: as was mention at the outset of this book. We pointed out a few of those signs earlier, that suggested, our Founding Fathers laid the foundation, if nothing else, for a *moral form of Government*. During that time in history, *"Theocratic"* was not the name used a lot in Government; but its definition was "implied" in our laid out of the laws of the land.

In the Bible, the English name Theocratic wasn't the name used either. But...this was the only type of Government enforced in the Bible with those men God chose to lead nations.

The feeling of God being the sovereign ruler over our nation, started to be recognize by adding "one nation under God" to our "Pledge allegiance of the Flag" in 1954. But less than ten years later...Prayer...that was usually associated with the "Pledge Allegiance of the Flag," in the start of the School day in every America school; was remove(1962). This was the start of the demoralization of America..."removal of Prayer".

The fact that this book has proved, that the Same Sex Relationship issue is a religious matter...has open the door for the *"Theocratic Party"*. By using President Theodore Roosevelt first name as a basic for the *"Theocratic Party"*, we will start seeing results within three years of its initiation. This was the number of years, after Theodore Roosevelt became President, that the Wright brother successfully flew. If Obama is the last Democratic Party President; then it stand to reason, that the *"Theocratic party"* is its best replacement.

A little more history of the name Theocratic, suggest that "Theo" is Greek for God and "crat" taken from "kratos" means power. This "God Power"...*Theocratic party*, is the antidote for the *"Democratic-Demon create"* atmosphere; that is now corrupting our nation on a daily basic.

As pointed out earlier, "Atmosphere" is what causes our thought process. A Religious Political Party like *"Theocratic"*; will start conditioning the atmosphere...causing the nation leaders to come up with solutions that would put us back on track and keep us on track. President Abraham Lincoln's, first *Republican* President, put us on track and kept us their for one hundred years. The *Theocratic* party will do the same and longer. This Party name is the Salvation and destiny of America.

The *Theocratic Party*, based on the name Theodore Roosevelt contribute to the success of the Wright Brothers Historical Flight; also, made the atmosphere conducive for the rapture or the *"second coming of Christ"*. Because...in the name airplane, is a subliminal message with three words...air-plan-e...the "e" at the end means just that..."end". So airplane interprets as *"Air plan end"*. The "Second Coming of Christ"(Rapture) is the *"Air Plan"* that will come at the *"end"*.

God is giving us a choice with the *Theocratic party*. We can create this party to minimize the evil in our nation, or...allow God to do it in Earthquakes, Tornadoes or the most thorough job.... mass Baptism; we call Flood. Or God can just use the "Bundle method" and send a "Tsunami".

After Noah's flood, God promise he would not destroy the earth again with a flood. As a token to that promise, the Rainbow that appears after some of our rain storm reminds him of that promise(*Genesis 9:11-17*). In reading that verse, it said: *"he would not destroy the earth"*, he didn't say he wouldn't take out a Nation like America...on earth.

During the 2005 Katrina Storm, he prove he would take out a "State by flood" and assume, he will take out a Nation like America if need be. One of the reason he said he wouldn't destroy the earth with a flood again; because he would initiated a more humane plan: call Baptism...in the New Testament. Meaning people would be responsible for symbolically washing away there own sins. As a nation, we haven't kept faithful to that plan either; do we wouldn't have so many states with flood problems.

By the way...done with the right mind set; Baptism is the permanent cure for Homosexuality

When the virtue or grace has been driven out of the land by corruption of sin, it causes a crack in the earth...we call earthquake. When lewd sexual activities, like Homosexuality, has gotten out of hand in large cities...driving out the good spirit... this is what causes earthquakes. The Bible speak of *earthquakes in divers places*(*Matthew 24:7*). Divers means "difference places". This is saying places that earthquakes does not normally hit. With Same Sex Marriage legal all over the nation; you can expect earthquakes are going to hit in places never hit before(*divers*).

By this lifestyle going against nature, it is driving out the Good spirit or energy. The good Spirit is the glue or cement that holds the world together. It is the *"Salt"* of the earth mention earlier. If the Homosexual behavior is driving out the Good Spirit in our nation, where do you think this "Good Spirit" is going? If it is going out on a *National level daily, another nation could be absorbing it. That nation will eventually get powerful enough to rise up against us* if we doesn't get control of the publicity of Homosexuality. This type of "Nation take over" will be a lot worse than 911.

The *"Theocratic party"* is the Solution for today. For more than fifty years, America has flirted with a need for a new party. Names have been suggested, but none has stuck to make a difference in an election. The Political climate in our nation is just begging for a new political party. The reason no party has stuck, is because, it is not the party names that our atmosphere and God is demanding.

It took a new party to end Slavery, and it will take a new party to put Homosexuality back in its rightful place. The Democrat and Republican party cannot do it, because they feeds the Homosexual atmosphere in soliciting their votes in elections.

The origin of the Republican party was to stop the spread of Slavery. With that philosophy, God caused it to win an election with a man's first name of Abraham. A Biblical name, that took on a Bible purpose...ending servitude. And now, we are at the cross road of destiny again.

One of the qualification of a leader for the *Theocratic party*; he got to know God. Not in a preaching, church type of way; but in a political way as President Abraham Lincoln. It was hard for President Lincoln to make a speech without using some Bible reference.

The Theocratic party will allow every Religion to practice equally. This party will not destroy the first Amendment on freedom of religion, it will fulfill it.

In *I Samuel 8:7-9* when Israel ask for a king, instead of a Prophet; God told Prophet Samuel to give the people what they wanted. This was the beginning of America's Democratic style of Government...*of the people, by the people and for the people.* Nowhere in history did I discover I founding father were aware this.

After Israels' requested for a King, God chose Saul as first King, and told prophet Samuel to anoint him. By doing that, this Democrat Government becomes a Theocratic Government.(*I Samuel 9:16-27& 10:1*) This means, with a Theocratic Government in America; it will pick the right man for the position of President in each election, automatically.

Our Constitution points out, that a President does not have to be subject to a Religious test. But with the *Theocratic Party*, it will not only pick the right man by the people, it will generating the right thought process, on knowledge of how to run this type of Government effectively. This would be mostly done by the first President elected under the *Theocratic Party*...like President Lincoln done with Slavery; as the first President of the Republican party.

The Republican Party was born to stop the spread of Slavery. And it did..."it stop it permanently". The same as the Theocratic

Party will do to Homosexuality. The Theocratic Party wouldn't only end the publicity of Homosexuality; but help control other evils that are destroying our country as well. Like Racism, nothing will ever completely vanquish Racism on earth, but can reduce the publicity of it, from where it is today in America.

We mention earlier, how the *Theocratic party* will destroy the evil that the Democratic party and name for our Government has created...a *"demonic atmosphere"*. Also, how this *"Demon Created"* atmosphere from our Government title of Democracy; has created a spirit of confusing by demonic deception. And our greatest deception and confusion, thus far, in our nation and the world, is deceiving people out of their "anatomy birth identity". This confusing is making a birth male believe he is a female, and birth female desiring sexually another female. The greatest evil that the Democratic Atmosphere has robbed us of, is our "Superior male".

Because of our love of Super heroes, it should be a far gone conclusion, that America suppose to produce a Superman-Superhuman in the form of Hollywood's fictitious Superman. It is my believe, that Benjamin Franklin kite lightning experiment(1752) brought down from the heavens a Superhuman spirit with it. Twenty four years after this event(1752) a nation was born(1776)... America. I interpret this "twenty four" year period, as number of "hours in a day"; with an interpret conclusion of...the "Sign of the TIME"...when our nation was born.

It was in God's plan for this nation to evolved a real live, honest the Goodness, Superman. The process of bringing this Superhuman to life was initiated with our first television series of Superman in 1952.

The reason I used Benjamin Franklin kite lighting experiment as the birth of the Spirit for our Superman, because the comic book symbol of Superman "S" on the chest is within a Kite symbol. The author of that symbol, created it as a Diamond shape...with good rationale. In his vision-idea of the Superman character, he saw the basic form of the "S" on the chest; that he interpret within a Diamond shape. That was the shape he was familiar with. To him, Superman is a fictitious character. But with me, Superman is a reality. In thinking that way, logic dictated to me that this power came down during Franklin kite-lighting experiment. The Diamond make sense also...describing the uniqueness and the value of that man chosen for this place in history. *Isaiah 13:12* describes Superman like this: *I will make a man more precious than fine gold;even a man than the golden wedge of Ophir.* Of course, during that time in Bible history, it was referring to an elect child of God, mainly, Jesus the coming Messiah.

Of course Hollywood, for entertainment purpose, try to give a logical explanation for the "S" in their creation of Superman. But that is actual a kite shape that "S" is within on the chest of the Superman's costume. That "S" has several meaning; "Spirit" "Super" "Superior" or "Savior" etc...all at the same time when viewed.

In the same year and month(September 1952) that a fictional character premier to play the role of Superman; God birthed the man who was born to be the real Superman in America. This came as a result of Franklin kite-lighting experiment 200 years earlier(1752). With the perfection of the number 200; I took that as having a divine meaning. But because mistakes where made in the origin of America(1789) with our first President; this plan did not happen. For the details of who this first Superman was suppose to be; reference the book, *"The Half Have Never Been Told"* *by Jolomark Retunah.*

We notice this Superman persona all around us, especially in Sports. Also, when you have modern day actors/actresses doing their own stunts; they are embracing their Superhuman side. The details of Superman in the above mention book, states that he has to be, biologically, a whole man...balancing both the female and the male within him. This is what makes him a God. This would make him like Adam, before God's rib surgery creating Eve.

Jesus laid the foundation for this modern day superman by performing Supernatural miracles during his three year ministry. Hollywood has demonstrated what a modern day Savior-Superman would be capable of. Believe it or not, I have taken you down this road to let you know, many men that are "Gay", where born to be a Superman. But "Demonic confusing" has taken them over, resulting in Homosexuality in the form of "transgender".

The evil has attacked God's first creation man and turn him into an "Abomination" in America. The greatest of these Abomination is Bruce Jenner-Caitlyn Jenner. Here is a man that demonstrated the capabilities of a Superman at the World's Olympic(1975) and turned God's Glory into an *"Abomination"*. Rather than embracing the female part of himself, making him a "God", he gets confuse and become an *"Abomination"*. This is like a man hitting the Big lottery and misplace...NO...and loose...the lottery ticket. And for him to be rewarded for becoming transgender, is an even bigger Abomination for "all" involved. This is the work of our *"Democratic-Demon Create"* atmosphere.

Before becoming transgender, earlier in that year, Bruce Jenner was in a car accident and someone was killed. The headline later that year read; **"Bruce Jenner could be charge for Man Slaughter".** What an appropriate headline; considering he change his sexual identity from a man to a woman. Was that a play on words by God and the Universe? According to the scripture, he really is charge with **"man slaughter"** in the eyes of God.

The truth of the matter is that, God wasn't just going to create a Superman in America. The plan was to create a Super Race of People. Which would probably involve all these Gay men in America of today. Adolf Hilter of Germany, had this idea first, but the Devil confused him in another way. He had him to take God's chosen people; the Jews, torture and kill them. He was suppose to be embracing God's chosen; instead, the Devil confused him and he killed them.

On the day that Hitler was to demonstrate a specimen of his Super Race of people; God took the *"Super race Birthright"* from Germany, and gave it to America. Because...up to that point in History, America was keeping close to the right moral path... closer than other nations.

Germany loosing their Super race birthright was done through Jesse Owens winning four(4) Gold Metals in the 1936 Olympics. Hitler's was so disgusted of Jesse Owens ability, on one event, he gets up and walk out of the stadium. (I recommend watching the recent movie "Race" featuring the life of Jesse Owen).

God took the Birthright from one country(Germany) of a chosen victimize people(the Jews) and gave it to another country(America) with a chosen victimize people(the Negro). For the way Jesse Owens was treated by America after this; it slowed us down as a Nation for this Super race of people once again.

After this, in America, it is reveal how the devil work in the mind of men with deception through Homosexuality. The man look at his body and the Devil says *"you are not surely a man". Referencing the scripture: Genesis3:4...And the serpent said unto the woman, Ye shall not "surely die"...* All these Gay men and women in America, that could have been Super humans are now *Abominations.*

I discovered years ago, the more important you are, the worse the Devil try to make you look. When you are describe as a Homosexual, this makes it almost impossible, for you to come back from this and do something meaningful for mankind.

If you doesn't believe that this nation was destine to created a Super Race of people, consider this piece of History if you would.

Before the thirteen colonies became a nation, there was a story told, as a prophecy, about George Washington being the leader of a powerful nation. An Indian Chief visited George

Washington during the British American War before we obtained our Independence. He told George Washington that he wanted to meet the man first hand, who would never die in battle and that would reign over a Great Nation. This is his explanation of why he said that to the future first President of America:

Note: The incident described below is when America was still under British rule as the thirteen colonies.

The Indian Chief told George Washington; that during one of the Wars where Washington was leading a militia during an Indian and British War, the Indian chief told his best marksman to take careful aim at the leader(Washington) on the White horse. The Indian Chief's marksman took careful aim at Washington during this battle and shot at him four(4) different times. The Indian Chief said Washington never failed off the horse, nor never was he struck by the bullets. George Washington responded to the Indian chief immediately, and said, "yes...I remember that day". "Because...that was the day my horse was shot from under me three times and when the day was over I had three bullets holes in my clothes". (quote is from a video, "our Godly Heritage" by the "Wallbuilders")

This means that George Washington as first President; life, would set the standard and tone of this nation and its inhabitants. Meaning that, not only would George Washington supernatural persona, set the tone for all presidents that seceded him; but the people of future Generation in America as well. In retrospect...it appear; that today, as a nation and its leaders, "all" has become confused.

This nation has been struggling against an evil that was of our own making with "democracy" since its origin. Every-time we almost loose the battle with evil, God manage to send us the right person or persons. It's not always through a President. It can be through others whom has taken their fame and use it for Good.

But now, with the legalization of Same Sex Marriage, we are very close to loosing this battle against evil. With men sleeping with men and women with women the atmosphere is very messed up. All this immorality is coming from the top of the Nation. The President, The Supreme Court, outspoken celebrities and the lack of Preaching the Gospel by Mega Church Ministers.

It is a noted thing, that when you are the best, everybody wants a shot at you. Many nations has risen up against us and we defeated them. And some of those nations leaders recognize our Sovereignty and become our ally. But now we have factions, different organization and small groups trying to take us down as a Nation. They are doing it with the weapon that made us a Great and powerful Nation. That is through our strong and dominating Religious beliefs.

Nineteen men, with a belief in their God and his reward, left an eternal mark of destruction on our country because of our "moral decay". We call this eternal mark of moral decay...911. By initiating the *Theocratic* party. we will not have to depend on the Gospel being preached by misguided ministers. This Political party will create the right atmosphere automatically and we will stay on course.

The 911 disaster proved, we are vulnerable; despite having the greatest weapon arsenal in the world. It was said by Osama Bin Laden before he initiated the 911 attack: "America is not as strong as they use to be". He knew our arrogance had made us vulnerable. But the *Theocratic* party will make us great again. I am assured by high authority in the writing of this book; if we correct this Same Sex Marriage problems, our "rewards" are just as equal as the consequences of not correcting it.

Nation's Reward for Homosexual Containment

The one thing that we have not discussed in detail about getting the Homosexual problem under control, is the reward that the nation will be granted for doing this. That is probably a very unusual statement to be making. A reward...for stopping an evil that has been legalized by the Government. Its been done before.

We have dealt with a number of Bible evils in this country and never recognize the rewards that the nation receive for handling them properly. When I discovered the reward the nation will receive for handling this issue properly; I finally answer the big question that has bothered me for years.

Why didn't Jesus deal with the Same Sex issue during his three year ministry on earth?

The Gay community, and their supporters believe....because there is no record of Bible history of Jesus dealing with this issue, it was not a sin...but that is not the case.

If Jesus time on earth was to deal with all man's problem, he wouldn't have chosen twelve Disciples-Apostle to spread his message of Salvation, after his ascension. Jesus major purpose, was to be an eternal Sacrificial lamb for man's sins. The forerunner of Christ...John the Baptist; who paved the way for Christ's ministry support this fact. *John 1:29 The next day John seeth Jesus coming unto* *him, and saith, Behold the **Lamb** of God, which taketh away the sins of the world.* John the Baptist baptized Jesus under that revelation. **Lamb** being one of the most popular sacrificial animal for sin in OT law.

Furthermore, during Jesus earthly ministry, they were still under OT law and the Same Sex issue wasn't a problem. Because, the death penalty that went with this practice was severely enforced. Not to mention, they took the historical destruction of Sodom and Gomorrah very serious. Nobody was going to be making any public confession(coming of the closet) about being Gay, like they are doing in America today. Also, Jesus was dealing with issue during his ministry as they came about. The NT did not come into play until Jesus ministry ended...with his death, burial, resurrection and ascension.

To prove they were still under OT law was when the people brought a woman to Jesus *caught in the very act of Adultery. (John 8:1-11)* The first thing the mob brought to the attention of Jesus is what OT Law said..."STONE HER". If the OT Law said kill someone for a sin, the town was ready to do that. When the synagogue hypocrites brought the woman to Jesus "caught in the act of adultery", they came with their stones as wells. It didn't matter whether the mob that brought the adulterous woman had done an equal or worse sin, they were ready to follow OT law. No one had caught any of the mob in their sins; so they were okay in killing someone that was caught. Asking the mob about their own sins, was the way Jesus diffused the situation.

Nevertheless, the Apostles, mainly Paul...dealt with the Same Sex issue in NT style. Paul represented the Gentiles...all non Jewish People. The Apostle Paul...being sometimes nickname "The Gentile Savior" in modern day Bible teaching, was dealing with this problem for us of today. As you can see...America...a dominating Gentile nation, and the greatest nation on earth, is the main nation promoting Same Sex Marriage. You doesn't hear America's ally Israel of today, having a Homosexual problem.

Because, the history of their nation *name* is founded upon OT law. They are familiar with all the laws pertaining to Same Sex Marriage and the consequences.

We have listed all the NT Scriptures pertaining to the Same Sex issues in this book by Paul and the other Apostles. Ultimately, Jesus had a much greater plan of how to handle issues such as this on a mass scale.

God's ultimate plan was to set aside a place on earth to deal with all unfinished Bible issues. The place would be called the United States of America.

America became the testing and proving ground of OT Law and NT Scripture. The various Religion's in American covers either one or both (OT and NT) of these sections of the Bible, thoroughly.

I have come to understand, after reading the Bible; if man messes up, then man is responsible for his own mess. Whether man messes up individually as a person, or collective as a nation-world, the problem has to be corrected by the like. God's role is this: if you are willing and obedient, he will give you opportunity, knowledge, and the tools to help you correct the problem.

This is what he done in the days of Noah. He didn't create another man and woman nor animals; he just chose the most Righteous branch of humans. Within Noah's family, would be three men(Noah's sons) with wives, that would produce three differ family types to repopulate the world. Also, Noah was responsible for getting two of every animal male and female for reproduction in a New world. This was the way that God first corrected man's mistake of a whole world.

After Jesus came; God decided to start cleaning the original mistakes of man both the first world of Adam and Eve and the Second world after Noah's flood. America would be God's test of

Jesus New Testament that he created in the Bible. A land was set aside from the days of Noah to prepare a people for his Glory. Our nation...God set aside; would be responsible for taking care of some major problems that was initiated in the Bible.

After the water receded from this special land preserve from Noah's flood; a man would be birthed who would discover this land. This man will be so named that he would not miss his purpose in providing the first phase of God's final experiment. This man was name Christopher Columbus.

Christopher Columbus understood America's purpose before he discover the land. Listen to what he said to the "Investors" of his voyage...King Ferdinand and Queen Isabella of Spain in 1502... ten years after his discovery of America.

"In the carrying out of this enterprise of the Indies, neither reason nor mathematics nor maps were any use to me; fully accomplished were the words of Isaiah".

Isaiah 11:11,12 *And it shall come to pass in that day, that the Lord shall set his hand again the second time to recover the remnant of his people, which shall be left, from Assyria, and from Egypt, and from Pathros, and from Cush, and from Elam and from Shinar, and from Hamath, and from the islands of the sea. And he shall set up an ensign for the nations, and shall assemble the outcasts of Israel, and gather together the dispersed of Judah from the four corners of the earth.*

In that verse Isaiah described the whole earth. Some how of another, Columbus knew that scripture was telling him that all the land covered by water during Noah's flood did not recede at the same time. There was something out there beyond the sea line that was waiting for him.

Columbus discovery of America was based on religious principles. Although the King and Queen had religious beliefs, Columbus couldn't based his rationale for their financial backing totally on a Scripture from the Bible. He had to tell them what they wanted to hear. In other words, before he could sail, he had to sell...the King and Queen on the mission.

For any historians, who doubt the name Christopher Columbus is the rightful discoverer of America, we hope we can put that to rest, right now as well with his name interpretion.

First, the complete title and name of our Savior is "Christ Jesus". In likeness, with the name *"Christ*opher"... our Saviors title *"Christ"* is in the first part of his name Christ-opher.

From the last name Columbus, we take the word *"us"* from the end of his name that parallels the end of the name Jes*us ;* and later to be the Acronym US(United States): connecting all the lands in this given peninsula.

After Christ Jesus blessed this land or marked it; all was needed was for Christopher Columbus to recognize his destiny. The above Isaiah scripture helped him do that. The land would draw him to it because of the above "Christ Jesus" interpretation from his name(*Christ*opher Columb*us)*. In other words, he became a "Human Compass" in discovering this New World Blessed by "Christ Jesus".

This information on our land discovery, by Christopher Columbus, is simply, to validate our religious heritage and how this land lines up with the Bible.

After people began to migrate to this land; another part of the God's plan unfolded. That was the power to run this great nation. This was done by Benjamin Franklin kite-lighting experiment. In that experiment, the knowledge and power to create an Awesome nation was activated.

The discovery of electricity in Franklin experiment, brought with it, the atmosphere to build a Godly nation. This atmosphere would create "Names" for the present and future children to build this nation. This atmosphere guided men to the Holy Bible to help with the details of this nations' mission.

As the children were being expose and taught from the most popular book in America...the Bible; all the contents of the Bible begin to be put in the nations atmosphere.

The Bible saturation of the atmosphere would guide us to know what was good and what was Evil. God's plan is enforced. To prove the affects of the Bible atmosphere, go back in history, and view how appropriate our First presidents and vice-presidents names were to start us on the path for a nation "Under God". To give clarity as to what the First President and vice-presidents name interprets reference *The Half Have Never Been Told.*

Once the nation was on the right path, the phrase "manifest destiny" started to be tossed around the nation. This was referring to the size of the nation: as well as its sovereignty. The pioneers begin to recognize that America was a chosen nation.

The first mission after the Nation was clearly defined, was to clean up the Institute of slavery. Some of the earlier American patriots recognize this, but not the main one....President George Washington.

He recognize this on a personal level; but not on a Nation level. Personal level, in that, he stipulated in his "Will", that his slaves be set free after him and his wife Martha had deceased.. but not the freedom of slavery on a National level.

President George Washington was suppose to make it his mission to free the slaves, as an appreciation to God for freeing the thirteen colonies from the tyranny of King George III. Because he fail to do this, is probably the reason the Almighty gave him such a short Post President life. He died less than three years after leaving office. He was only 67 years of age. Very short...when you compare 35 years of post President life of Ex President Jimmy Carter...who is still alive.

George Washington not freeing the slaves as the first president; is what stopped the Superman process from happening mention above(1952) initiated by Ben Franklin kite-lighting experiment(1752).

Because President George Washington did not free the Negro slaves, it took eighty seven years for the nation to achieve the first phase of God's plan. Although, America got behind in their first "spiritual" mission, they didn't get behind in their "physical" mission as a nation. For example, the "Louisiana Purchase" double the size of the United State at the time it was purchased.

Because the First President dropped the ball on freeing the Slaves; this caused, Abraham Lincoln and George Washington to be born in the same month. This is why, later in history, February has been celebrated as President month.

Lincoln put the nation back on track by freeing the Slaves. In a two and half minute Speech(*The Gettysburg Address*); Lincoln sum up the purpose of America up until that time.

I stated above, that God allows man the tools to clean up his own mess. The reason that the Gettysburg Address was so profound and one of history's greatest speeches is because of the train ride. The riding on the train as Lincoln drafted the speech was literally putting the whole nation back on "track". (*The train and tracks is one of the tools mention above God gave man to correct the first Presidents mistakes*). This is also why the "Gettysburg Address" is an eternal document. President Lincoln was literally... on Historical "track" when he wrote it.

It took at least ten years after the Emancipation Proclamation was signed for all Slaves in America to be freed; and even then, it still wasn't over for many slaves. After the slaves freedom, God begin to reward the Nation by giving the "Industrial Revolution" a differ appearance. This was started by the invention of the telephone and the light bulb. These two gifts of God could be consider as Bible metaphors or reference scriptures from the Bible about our nation. For example, the invention of the telephone could mean we are the "message" to the world. Or...*Many are "call" but few are chosen(Matt.22:14) And the invention of the light bulb...Ye*(we) *are the "Light" of the World"...A city that sit on a Hill(U.S. Capitol) cannot be hid.(Matt. 5:14-16)*

To add credence; that these are gifts from God to the Nation for freeing the slaves are these quoted words by President Lincoln: *"as long as we have slaves we enslave ourselves."* The freedom of the slaves from their bondage, released the blessings of American from its bondage as well. Also, by looking at the Birth of the two inventors...Bell and Edison; in relation to the Emancipation Proclamation, is another clue as the nation gifts for freeing the Slaves.

Alexander Graham Bell born March 3, 1847 inventor of the telephone and Thomas Edison inventor of the light bulb was born February 11, 1847. As you can see, these two pioneer inventors are born almost a month apart. These two major inventors were clearly, waiting in the wings for God to release the power for their inventors talents through the slaves freedom. These two inventors were teenagers when the Emancipation Proclamation was initiated. And after the slaves freedom, their gifts of the telephone and light bulb manifested on a world wide scale.

But the real success of the telephone did not need a Bible metaphor. This was the prelude to the telephone...the telegraph; invented by Samuel F.B Morse. He knew what being able to communicate at a distant meant. So he took a scripture with four very powerful words and open a pathway into the "Supernatural". These Miraculous, very magical and Supernatural words, were taken from *Numbers 23:23...*"WHAT HATH GOD WROUGHT!"... the very first words; transmitted successfully over the telegraph.

Samuel Morse recognize this gift from God. Those four words holds the secret to all communication and transportation invention of the world following this invention. Also in the same year(1837) of the "Telegraph Invention" the first Steam Engine for a "Train" was built. Meaning that man is begin to realize they can move from place to place without walking...the use of horses.... donkeys and mules.

It will be revealed, that those four powerful words; first transmitted over telegraph, open the door for two of the greatest invention of mankind...not invented yet; that this nation will receive: IF...WE/US...just get this Homosexual problem under control.

Along with the freedom of the Slaves, as the nations first big accomplishment; this freedom was also felt around the world. It was felt by a Frenchman by the name Fre'de'ric Auguste Bartholdi the creator of the Statue of Liberty. Although New York wasn't the original plan for the Statue...the Statue of Liberty did find God's destiny for it. This was a gift from God...for the nation: from a foreign land; proving...that the world is recognizing our Sovereignty.

Forty years after the Emancipation Proclamation, America could fly. In 1903, the Wright brothers achieve flight...another Gift from God. God made it crystal clear that this was a Gift to our nation. Because...the historical flight of the Wright Brothers took place December 17th 1903...eight days before Christmas. The number "eight": because of Noah's family of eight, is known as the number of "New Beginning." The Wright Brothers gave the nation's mascot...the Eagle...the power to fly.

Take a look at the Wright Brothers birthdays. Wilbur was born April 16, 1867; four years after the Emancipation Proclamation of the slaves. Orville Wright was born August 19, 1871 eight years after the Emancipation Proclamation. At this point, most of the Slaves nationwide had been freed. Total freedom had to be in the atmosphere because flying, represent the greatest freedom of all. So God release these two Angels from Heaven to America, to bring about the greatest creation of mankind...the gift of Flight. I am sure that their father being a devout Minister didn't hurt either.

Giving America the Gift of Flight eight days before Christmas; is like Santa Clause bringing the Nation a Toy. If you look at the Gifts God Gave America; it make a lot of sense, why Christmas is the favorite Holiday of the majority of Americans. With God's first gift to the world..."His Son"; he added a lot of Gifts to America. We think that the "Christmas Carol" lyrics whose *naughty or nice* is just for the children...it is for the adults as well.

The publicity of Homosexual, is of course, on God's naughty list for America. To prove this, is what was mention earlier about the slaughtering of those 20 children of Newtown, Connecticut at Sandy Hook Elementary. This act was done eleven days before Christmas. We know that Children are the greatest recipient of Christmas. This was more than just a "lump of Coal" in America's Christmas Stocking. This event coming at the end of the year; in the month of our nations biggest holiday, greatly displayed God's Anger. And for what reason...publicizing Homosexuality.

Most of America's great Gifts are the results of freeing the Negro Slave. When Lincoln freed the slaves, we were back on Bibles course. He ended the long time curse of Servitude of Canaan: by his gran father Noah. This was the defeat of a Great Evil. Lots of blood was shed in the Civil War to stop several thousand years of this evil. Keep in mind, every time we defeat evil, we are rewarded individually as a person and collectively as a nation.

As mention earlier...the Civil War rid the nation and world of a great evil. In ridding the world of that evil, we also unknowingly created an equal or worst evil later in history.....Homosexuality.

Nevertheless, we hope that you are convinced that God did rewards us for taking care of the evil of servitude-slavery.

Following the Negro slaves freedom, another freedom was being achieved in America. The woman was on the path toward receiving her right to vote. This becomes the second major issue for the birth of America to correct for mankind. This is why the "freedom" that the "Statue of Liberty" represent is the face of a Woman. This freedom for the woman is pertaining to the first sin activated by Eve in the Garden of Eden.

The historical move of "Women Suffrage" takes us back to the Garden of Eden: starting the process of the woman regaining her lost of equality to her husband.

When our first President dropped the ball on freeing the slaves in America; we lost the great honor of inventing the first car. If you look at history of the automobile in America, when we invented our version of the horseless carriage it ran close to the invention of the Airplane. We were barely getting the hang of traveling without the use of horses and mules on the ground, when the Wright brothers took to air in flight. Meaning that, although the automobile got behind in its invention; the Wright Brothers were right on time with there Gift to the world.

Henry Ford was not the original inventor of the automobile. However, in creating his version of the car, he perfected the "Assembly Line". This gave the world something equally as important as the first Automobile. By man being a co-creator with God, this gave man a simpler way to mass produce any creation or invention man came up with. This also increase mass production and kept the nation-world employed.

As we are relating these gifts from God, to the freedom of slavery and women suffrage; actually, the Negro slave wasn't completely freed until the passing of 1964 Civil Rights Bill. And after this achievement, American got another reward. Not only were we first in flight by the Wright brothers, we were first to put a man on the moon. This also took place in the same decade, of the passing of the Civil Rights Bill.

With the acceptance of integration in our nation and around the world, technology is improving in every facet of American living as well. Just because we are doing the right things.

Whether its individually as a person, or collectively as a nation, when we "delay" to do the right thing; that cost us sometimes, as much as not doing the right thing. To support that philosophy; when George Washington fail to freed the Negro Slave during his two terms as President, it cost the nation one hundred years. Yes...that's correct...one hundred years.

Many are familiar with the one hundred year parallel of President Kennedy life with that of Abraham Lincoln. There are as many as fifteen to twenty parallels of these two men life and Presidency one hundred years apart. (Reference the book *"The Half Have Never Been Told"* for the details of some of those parallels). Two things happening a like, is considered a coincidence, but with that many parallels...our creator is trying to tell us something important.

The message of these parallels one hundred years apart is the results of George Washington not freeing the slaves as "first President". This is "how" George Washington delay on the slaves freedom cost the nation "one hundred years" of advance technology. If Washington would have freed the Slaves....when Lincoln became President, he would have sign the Civil Rights Bill instead of the Emancipation Proclamation. And John Kennedy would have been speaking of Life in space or living on other Planets rather than putting a man on the Moon in his Inaugural Address.

Because of this massive blunder by our first President; God, created a third power in our Nation. For centuries, the two most powerful tools that guided a society was the Church and the Government. But America has a third influential group of people as mention earlier...the entertainment industry...we call Hollywood.

Through special affects, the film industries is able to create things man fantasize over... that actually inspire "Reality". For example, during the 60's of the original "Star Trek" series; the "flip cell phone" was introduce wireless and non-stationary...thirty years later became a reality. The catchy mission statement of Star Trek "To Boldly go where no man has gone before" actually paid off. The "Star Trek" series was when Hollywood was on track and knew their mission. Not like the "Hollywood" of today pushing the ungodliness of Same Sex Marriage...messing everything up.

We have listed many gifts from God, for the nation as a whole doing the right thing. But because of this third power... Hollywood...the nation hasn't had a "World Changing Invention" in a long time.

In the last year (2016) of President Obama term in office he was touting on a talk show his accomplishments during his two terms. He mention promoting the legalization of Same Sex Marriage as one of them. This is not a world changing event. This Presidential action...by now, I hope that you can see; has the potential of ushering in the Genocide of America.

The film industry flirts with a lot of great ideas; just for entertainment. When in fact many of them can be a reality. The only thing we are doing alone the line of invention in today's world, is improving, already invention from early Pioneer Americans. For example, bringing the telephone from a stationery tool to a mobile hand held computer device. Household appliance, outdoor equipment...like farming; is just being modified. And the automobile, is just being improved for safety. The automobile needs to fly or hover; like in the movies; to reduce every day traffic jams in the big cities. Pertaining to transportation, me being terrible at directions; I have to admit, GPS is one of the greatest inventions of modern time.

If Benjamin Franklin...Samuel Morse...Alexander Graham Bell...Thomas Edison...Henry Ford...the Wright Brother or other pioneer inventors, would have got the idea of Teleportation and Time Travel; these would not be a Block buster hit at the movies; they would be a working reality. And also, these Super heroes movies; with the ultimate human Superman, wouldn't be entertainment; they would be reality. We can have many of these things that the movie theater call entertainment...a reality.

Teleportation and Time Travel are gifts we can expect to receive if this nation will shut down the publicity of Same Sex Marriage. Again...this *"Abomination"* of Same Sex couples is messing up the atmosphere. Personalizing Same Sex Relationship, by keeping it to yourself and in the privacy of your bedroom...becomes an individual problem. But when it is publicized as law; it affects the whole nation through contaminating the atmosphere. As long as I continue to write this message I will not get tired of repeating that statement of fact.

The institute that is promoting Same Sex Marriage is the institute that is pushing "Fantasy" rather than "Reality". This is Hollywood and the entertainment industry. This evil of promoting Same Sex Marriage is killing the Faith that once motivated man to not only, "believe in the impossible", but "do the impossible". On the one hand, Hollywood is inspiring man for Great achievement and on the other hand, through pushing Same Sex Relationships, they are canceling out that inspirational progress.

What man has forgotten, regardless of the wisdom and knowledge used to create fiction or truth; all knowledge and wisdom comes from the same source. The question is: Do you tend to view this created knowledge as fiction or true. Our pioneer inventors view their inspiration knowledge and vision as a reality and pursued them with that results

Would you believe it, that the spread of Homosexuality and the issuing of Marriage licenses to Same Sex Couples is keeping us...the greatest nation on earth, from making the next great step for mankind? Believe it or not..."IT IS".

Rather than fantasizing with "Teleportation and Time Travel" we can actually achieve this. Do you know the number of angles the film industry has produced in movies and TV series about "Teleportation and Time Travel"? Lots of them. Belief it or not, with the right kind of Faith, those television-movie theories, could be realities.

I could be wrong on this, but to my knowledge, there was only one T.V. Series that produced an episode about going to the moon before America achieve this: "The Twilight Zone". So what is the problem of the reality of Teleportation and Time Travel? Hollywood's adamant's support on Homosexuality; is killing the reality of great achievements.

Earlier pioneers worked on an idea until it crystallize their Faith. Listen to what Thomas Edison had to say about the invention of the light bulb: "somethings got to work because I have tried ten thousand things that doesn't work." Regardless of how many things that wouldn't work, Edison still believed a positive end.

And listen to the last public words of the Activist Susan B. Anthony; after spending her whole life on Women suffrage: *"Failure is Impossible."* Although she didn't not live to see the passing of Women suffrage; she believed her work was NOT in vain. She took two very negative words in the English Language; "failure and impossible" with a two letter verb..."is"...and created a phrase powerful enough to break through impossible barriers.

And today, concerning Time Travel and Teleportation, the TV-Movie industry is only interest in how many different spends they can put on these two for entertainment. These two invention is what Samuel F. B. Morse laid the foundation for with those four Miracle Words: *"WHAT HATH GOD WROUGHT"*. If I had to guess, the feeling Samuel Morse had when he transmitted those words successfully over Telegraph; it would come close to something like this: "YOU AIN'T SEEN NOTHIN YET"....Time Travel and Teleportation.

Those four quoted Bible words, actually, can help understand how to created the "portal" or "worm hole" that Hollywood describes as necessary for the success of Teleportation and Time Travel.

Even I myself, have a basic idea of how to achieved both Teleportation and Time Travel. But I don't have the mechanical nor technological skills to create these. But I do know, both are possible. I do have the first part of these inventions. The word that will open the "worm hole" or "portal" for these achievement. I discovered it in the New Testament with one of Jesus' miracles.

In the Bible book of Job during his suffering he described this portal or wormhole in his understanding during his time. Listen to *Job 28:7,8:There is a path which no fowl knoweth, and which the vulture's eye hath not seen: The lion's whelps have not trodden it nor the fierce lion passed by it.* This is dimensional thinking by the patriot Job.

With the early pioneer inventors of America; God gave one man all the tools for an invention. But today, with the world's massive population growth; a major invention can be in several hands, and take much longer than earlier inventors for it to come to fruition.

Going from Horse and buggy after thousands of years, and leap to the horseless carriage(the automobile) is a far greater leap than going from a car to Teleportation: all the hard work has been done. Teleportation is just a matter of putting the telephone and the automobile together with a mechanical, scientific understanding. The only thing keeping us from making these type of advancement...you got it: public promoting the evil of Homosexuality.

Yes...I am blaming everything on Homosexuality; because men are being characterize by their "sexual orientation" rather than by their "talents and skills". Man's skills and creative Genius are being blotted out by giving in to the evil of Homosexuality.

Furthermore, the tools for bringing new things to life is what make man a co-creator with God. We are not giving God anything to work with. God just doesn't "poof" things into existent. Even Jesus demonstrated this to us, in his earthly pilgrimage. He always had something to work with before a miracle was wrought.

As I understand this: Teleportation is the ultimate form of transportation and Time Travel is the ultimate of the Airplane. Both these inventions requires the right atmosphere. By publicizing Homosexuality; the atmosphere is not pure enough or clean enough for these two world changing and "sacred" inventions. Just goes to show by *Homosexuality violating nature it affects nature around us.* The earlier invention was wrought because of the pureness of the atmosphere. But because of the Spiritual nature of manipulating space and time with Time Travel and Teleportation; this requires someone on the scale of Moses to get verbal permission to create these.

There may be one stipulation in these two inventions. Whereas, Teleportation will be and can be the invention for a nation and world; Time Travel will not be. Because of the complexity of Time Travel, of which the movie industry has done a splendid job of pointing out; everybody will not be privilege to Time Travel...not even the Government.

Jesus prove this when he only took Peter James and John on the mountain of Transfiguration.

Transfiguration was a "form" of Time Travel in Bible days. These scriptures; *Matthew 17:1-9,* proved that Jesus Time Traveled. The above mention three disciple witness Jesus talking with both Moses and Elias whom had been dead for centuries. Jesus commanded the three not to tell anyone what they had seen. Which I took to mean; Time Travel suppose to be a secret, allowed only, to the very privilege(Godly).

Nevertheless, if you think that Time Travel and Teleportation is impossible; listen to what Jesus told his Disciples. *John 14:12 Verily, verily, I say unto you, He that believeth on me, the works that I do shall he do also: and greater works than these shall he do;because I go unto my Father.* When he said, *"go unto my father"* that meant he was returning to the source of "All Power". Experiencing man in the flesh and seeing man through human eyes, Jesus grew to understand how big man's ego is. Jesus starts that verse with strong conviction; *"verily verily"*....by definition those word means *"Truly Certainly".* That is another one of the strongest Promise Jesus made to his followers. Then he says, *"He that believeth on me,".* We are not believing on him when we are violating both OT Law and NT Scriptures.

If the word of God worked for Samuel Morse(*WHAT HATH GOD WROUGHT*) with the telegraph, from the OT; I have just as must confidence in words Jesus spoke in the NT.

When speaking of doing the impossible with God(*Matthew 19:26 & Mark 10:27*); man of today has paraphrase that scripture another way; *"Man's extremity is God's opportunity".*

Everything has a price to it. I...throughout this book, is telling you the price it takes to get these things Nationally. And to add to the above "...*greater works than these shall he do*" let's look at the first miracle Jesus done after resurrection: Teleportation.

Read these scriptures: *John 20:19 & 26 ...when the doors were shut where the disciples were assemble for fear of the Jews came Jesus and stood in the midst....And after eight days again his disciples were within, and Thomas with them: then came Jesus, the doors being shut, and stood in the midst.* These scriptures are describing Teleportation.

Jesus also let them know, he was a physical being and not a Spirit when he materialized in front of them. I took that to mean, we can do that today: especially, when the scripture say *"the doors being shut"*. Of course, this achievement will requires us to evolve through several generation; FYI: we have already evolved these generations. We just need to get the atmosphere right.

Jesus achieved this, after being tortured on the Cross. He had the strong mental discipline to control that pain so he could resurrect making inventions like Time Travel and Teleportation possible for us of today.

When Jesus was crucified on the cross, he was demonstrating the ultimate of his earthly ministry. This included mind over matter through great discipline. To bring such creation of Teleporting and Time Travel in existence, will require a discipline differ from that of our earlier inventors. Because, these invention are controlling invisible properties of the universe, with mechanical ingenuity, at a much greater level than other inventions.

Earlier, we gave the Government Party that has the power to make the atmosphere conducive for Supernatural inventions such as this. That was through the Government party called *"Theocratic"*. Of which was taken from President Theodore Roosevelt name.

This party also has the power to take the power from Hollywood beliefs of *fantasy* and spread it back in the nation where it belong and create *Reality*.

The reason the *"Theocratic"* tool can take the fantasy of Hollywood and turn it into reality, is because... Hollywood is failing their mission by being the primary supporter and promoter of this ungodly behavior of Same Sex Relationships.

Nevertheless, Hollywood has the duty of our third major mission for our nations existence: that is, to create the perfect man in the likeness of Jesus. Hollywood call this modern day Savior... Superman.

For four generation; Hollywood has been working on bringing this character more life like. The Bible and the teaching of Jesus Christ has the knowledge for the Superman character. Listen to what the prophet Isaiah had to say pertaining to Superman in *Isaiah 54:17 No weapon form against thee shall prospers....* also, listen to what Daniel said in *Daniel 9:21... the man Gabriel...being cause to fly swiftly.* That scripture did not say the "angel Gabriel"... being caused to fly...it said "man". Gabriel is the description, of the angelic spirit the man's body have to incarnate to fly as a Superman. These pieces of Scripture gives everything needed to birthed a Superman in America...right down to the day of his birth...September 21ˢᵗ.

A minister once told me, if you can prove through the scripture that something is possible...it will be done. Go back through this book and look at those things I have prove through scripture, that has already been accomplish in America.

In the television series of "Smallville" it demonstrated a few characters of Superman similar to Jesus Christ: that I contribute to its ten successful season. One of the first thing they done was to make his best friend Black. Meaning, he is savior to all people. Giving him the character of humility, and despite how evil a person is, they deserve to be saved; is Jesus Christ's thinking. And by the Superman character keeping his identity a secret fulfills the *Philippians 2:7* scripture *But made himself of no reputation, and took upon him the form of a servant.* If the scripture says it could be done...it will be done...*on earth as in Heaven.*

But if men are going to keep getting confused and become "transgender" this is going to push our ultimate man farther into the future or never at all. Or worse, let another nation make these Supernatural Advancements for mankind. God took this Supernatural Birthright from one nation(Germany) and gave it to us. Are we going to let him take it from us and give it to another country? This is suppose to be an American achievement not another nation. Homosexual men...listen to me....STOP...letting the evil or Devil...Fool You!!!

Becoming a Superman could possibly be some Gay man's reward by taking control of his mind. Learning how to balance his masculine and feminine side equally. Think about this; Jesus only had *"female flesh"(Luke 1:35)* He didn't get Gay about it; instead, he tamed and controlled himself to walk on water. He was every sense of word *"A Momma's Boy"*. That is usually the Gay man biggest supporter...momma.

The interpretation of *"walking on water"* in todays world, is the same as Superman flying. To you Gay men, Jesus was only male in his physical anatomy. Other than that *"He thought as a God"*... which was for our example. We know he was male because he was *circumcised eight days after his birth(Luke 2:21).* Let's not forget the scripture that said: *he was tempted in all ways as we, yet without sin(Hebrew 4:15).* And to add to that scripture; he was surrounded by at least twelve men all the time, and didn't go Homosexual.

Because of the publicizing of Same Sex Relationship in the nation, a modern day Superman and other major inventions has been put on hold. Man is loosing his way because of this behavior. This was evidence with the recent movie where the movie director wrote the story where a man driving a car (Batman) defeated a man that could fly under his own power(Superman).

Although this was all fictitious; it sends a very bad message about our Spiritual decline. That is allowing a mortal man, to defeat the ultimate human...Superman....A God: *I have said, Ye are gods; and all of you are children of the most High(Psalm 82:6).* Jesus reference this very Scripture in the New Testament during his three year ministry on earth in *John 10:34 : Jesus answered them, is it not written in your law, I said, Ye are gods?* Jesus wasn't teaching us to be human; he was teaching us to be God-like. By him repeating this OT Law-scripture in the NT; he is saying: "PEOPLE YOU NEED TO BELIEVE THIS". Jesus use of the word "Law" meant that this is a documented fact. It is going to happen somewhere, somehow; to somebody with the right kind of Faith.

The Superman character has been around since the days of comic books in 1938; and being undefeated until the reason movie "Batman vs Superman". Although they put kryptonite in the movies as his Achilles heel; Jesus, the real Superman...defeated Death.

The Homosexual atmosphere is so damaging; man cannot even create a fictional story with God being victorious over evil anymore. Keep in mind, the Superman Character is the interpretation of our modern day Jesus Christ...our Savior.

We demonstrated through the name Democrat with the interpretation of *Demon Create,* how our Government title has encourage the evil of our land. We...also through the name *"Theocratic"* and its interpretation, showed how this could be, the antidote...to stop the evil in our nation.

Throughout this book, I have tried to provide Bible Scripture and key moments in American history to show our nation to be in peril because of Homosexuality. But despite all the things wrong in our country; God has always left us a way out. He have provided a very detailed scripture as to what to do as a nation to get us back on track. President Reagan read this scripture in one of his speeches. As you read this scripture, think about how powerful the first words:(WHAT HATH GOD WROUGHT) transmitted by Samuel Morse over the telegraph were. Listen to the message God left his chosen when they found themselves off track.

II Chronicle 7:14
If my people, which are called
by my name, shall humble themselves,
and pray and seek my face, and turn from
their wicked ways; then will I hear from
heaven, and will forgive their sin, and
will heal their land.

By enforcing the *Theocratic party* you are fulfilling that scripture. And furthermore, for those who doesn't believe the phrase *"call by my name"* can be referring to America...let me show you.

We established earlier that the "us" in Jesus is the acronym for "United States". The position of where the "us" is located in the name Jesus represent our place in Bible history. Just as "us" comes at the end of the name Jes**us**, so shall the nation to fulfill Jesus' work come at the end as "US"...United States. When we refer to the name Jesus; we are speaking of the NT. But we can relate the phrase *"call by my name"* speaking about America in the OT as well.

In the very first verse written in this Book: *Genesis 1:26 And God said, Let **"us"** make man in our image*...This "us" has a stronger message of being the United States. Because, in his image is referring to the "Superman" that America is responsible for bringing into existence.

To do this, we have to show how the phrase *"called by my name"* relates to the whole name of the United States America. The first two letters "Am" of America get's its root from God's first introductory name to man. *Exodus 3:14 ...And God said unto Moses, I AM THAT I AM: and he said, Thus shalt thou say unto the children of Israel, **I AM** has sent me unto you.* The **"Am"** from God's name "I Am" starts the word "<u>Am</u>erica/<u>Am</u>-erica". This "AM" is also the last name of God's name "I Am". So the "Am" in America make God our Father. Like fathers of today, give children their last name: God has done the same for <u>Am</u>ericans. Just as the "Israelite" was God's chosen in the above scripture, God wisely created another chosen people from that Scripture...US.

"I AM" becomes the power of God over our nation, because the "I" is found in Amer(I)ca. Each citizen in America is call "an Ameri<u>**can**</u>". The "I" in the word "America" letting each of us know, we *"can"*...achieve greatness, because the four letters at the end of Amer<u>**Ican**</u> says "I Can". This simply means, with the above Scripture, we can accomplish anything we put our mind too. Regardless of our Race or Gender, the majority of American's feel they are special and have a unique purpose.

Those last three letters in the word American..."Can"...was used in our greatest achievement...removing the servitude curse of <u>*Can*</u>aan. Although the name Canaan has six letters; it is only compose of three differ letters: "C-a-n". As an Ameri<u>*can*</u>; from the very outset; "Freedom" has been our greatest battle cry. That is because, we were destine as a nation, by name, to end the curse of servitude placed on Canaan, for the first act of Homosexuality.

From this, you can see the wisdom of God in making sure we stay on track as a nation. This help us understand that the above scripture is talking about United States(US) when it says *"call by my name."*

America was created from that Scripture; that scripture was not created from America.

That scripture was here thousands of years before this nation was born. My job is just to interpret it. He inserted his name and plan on a mass scale, in the name, chosen for our country. It was good, that our nation was named, when the Spirit of God ran purely and freely; causing the Ministers in earlier America to preach the unadulterated Gospel.

God has rewarded us for the Good that we do. And when we follow the word of God conscience or other wise, we are seeking God's favor and he rewards us with gifts. By us respecting the OT Law and NT scriptures, we are seeking God's favor.

Matthew 7:9-11: or what man is there of you,whom if his son ask bread, will he give him a stone? Or if he ask a fish, will he give him a serpent? If ye then, being evil, know how to give good gifts unto your children, how much more shall your Father which is in heaven give good things to them that ask him? When we take steps to remove the publicity of Homosexuality, we are asking for good gifts. I have just requested which ones in this chapter. These gifts have scripture to support their request.

I have found, that God's favor comes in accordance with our faithfulness and our discipline. Getting the Homosexuality of this nation under control will require a great amount of sacrifice and discipline...but it can be done.

The Summary, Conclusion and final Solution

Ecclesiastes 12:13 Let us hear the conclusion of the whole matter: Fear God, and keep his commandments: for this is the whole duty of man.

Publicizing Homosexuality and promoting Same Sex Marriage is not *"Fearing God"*. In fact, in doing this, you have already broken his *"commandments"* of OT Law and NT Scriptures.

So far, in this book, we have presented things, I am sure, that you couldn't have possibly believe that related to Homosexuality. The reason for that is, to make the point clear, that anything that promotes or create deep rooted evil; contributes to the darkness,Homosexuality is born from.

Not to be confused, our nation has dealt with lots of evils. Its just that, Homosexuality, is a different kind of evil; detrimental to our nation on a private and public level.

As we have tried to point out, being Homosexual is one thing, but discovering the cause is a differ thing. I hope it is clear that this is behavior born from something dark and evil. We concluded that the major darkness and evil in this nation is a racial hatred until death. This racial hatred is generated by two major races in America. The Black race and the White race.

A Black racist is no better than a white racist. Neither of them does any good to a society. Because these two races encloses all other races; by getting them to unify, we reduce the majority of racial hatred in the nation; in return, reduce the future of Homosexuality.

Also, as you may have notice, throughout this book, the *Leviticus 20:13* scripture is the nucleus of this whole message. Therefore, it is important in our conclusion, that we make this scripture "crystal clear".

I drew the conclusion, that President Obama's clarity on supporting Same Same Marriage, can almost be the subtitle of his second Presidential term, that started in 2013. Because...this turned out to be the year of the biggest push on legalizing Same Sex Marriage. Of which, that number year(2013) parallels with the numerical scripture in the Bible book of *Leviticus* (*20:13*) against Homosexuality. I interpret this to meant, a strong warning against publicizing Homosexuality in America of today.

To add fuel to this fire, of this observation; a little more than a month after President Obama's 2012 election; (December 14, 2012) the Hook Elementary School in Newtown Connecticut suffer the massacre of 20, six and seven year old children. At that time... Connecticut was the second State in the United States that had signed off on legalizing Same Sex marriage. This incident was like an omen for things to come in President Obama's second term. Because...in the following years(2013-2015); "Mass Murders" mounted up(274) more in one year(2015) than any other President in the history of the United States. Coincidence....I think not.

With many unexplained facts like this...this book has made it clear, that no one is judging Homosexuals. Personal judging *is forming an opinion or conclusion* and most of the time, without facts. If you say he talks like a female, therefore he is Gay...that is judging. She have "Tom boy" ways; she is a Dyke-Lesbian...that is Judging. But in both of these cases; if they admit and confess they are Gay...the *Leviticus 20:13* scripture applies: *If a man also lie with mankind, as he lieth with a woman, both of them have committed an abomination: they shall surely be put to death; their blood shall be upon them.*

That scriptures does not mention female Homosexuals. In the Old Testament, the word "man" was meant to include woman, because when God created man...woman was included: *Genesis 1:27; So God created man in his own image, in the image of God created he him: male and female "created <u>he them</u>"*.. Meaning...that if man is corrected, so is the woman. However, the NT makes it clear that God is against female Homosexuals as well *(Romans 1:26)*. The point is, this scriptures has already judged the Homosexual. Let's see how.

First, this scripture describes the act: *"If a man also lie with mankind*(same gender), *as he lieth with a woman"*...this is what Gays are confessing to when they "come out of the closet". Moses then describe "you" and anyone that commit such an act, as this...*an Abomination*. What most Gays doesn't realize; that when they "confess" this behavior, they are confessing to a crime in that Scriptures. If you doesn't believe it is a crime, listen to the punishment...."*they shall surely be put to death*". With the use of the word *"surely"*, it is clear cut, that this actions, not only carries a death penalty; but definitely, will be enforced. When that scriptures ends with: *"their blood should be upon them:* it means they bought this upon themselves. I have heard moderate day judges said those very words at a criminals sentencing. That scripture is not judging...that scripture is a "Judgment". The crime and the punishment is in the same verse. When it is Quoted; if your lifestyle fits that scripture, then the penalty follows. Heterosexual that support Homosexual, make themselves an accessory to this crime; with the same penalty of murder...Death.

I have taken you down the rode of Judging and Judgment of this scripture to inform you and this nation of a very critical situation. That is...when our ultimate Judges...The Supreme Court

163

Judges, legalized Same Sex Marriage; they put this WHOLE nation in jeopardy of that judgment in the *Leviticus 20:13* scripture. That above scripture makes it plain, with the word *"surely"*, that someone is going to pay for this sin in death. This is in reference to mass murder in America, at an alarming rate...fulfilling the Bloodshed, the *Leviticus 20:13* scripture implied!!!

When you deny the New Testament teaching against Homosexuality by Jesus' Christ chosen Disciples-Apostle; you are back to Old Testament Law. You doesn't have the luxury of Jesus sacrificial death for your sins...if you continue to sin. You only have that luxury, when you confess and not "willfully" sin anymore.

When Jesus became the "Eternal Human Sacrificial lamb" in the New Testament for sin...*replacing* "animal sacrifice for sin in Old Testament"; it meant, from that point on, some human sacrifice has to be made for sin in all cases.

Whether you believe in Jesus, the Bible or "Not"...the message is clear...sin carries a penalty. The penalty on Homosexuality is death. It matters not how comfortable you have grown with your overt Gay life, someone still has to pay for that sin. As long as you are in a Same Sex relationship, it is a sin, and the punishment is enforced. Whether you recognize the punishment or not.

By the end of July 2016, I had attended four funeral this year on my mothers side of the family. All where females. The three oldest funerals where of natural cause or terminal sickness. The oldest three funeral was still too young to die. But the funeral of the youngest was Blood shed which pertain to the *Leviticus 20:13* scripture. Because...her family support a "Same Sex Marriage".

This brings me to a lot of familiar phrases I have heard at these "Blood shed" funeral of the very young. For example.... "that is crazy". "That doesn't make sense"!!! These are "senseless" deaths. "That child never done anybody wrong." This is the big one at the young peoples Funeral; "WHYYY"..."Somebody PLEASE TELL ME WHYY"....."Lord help me understand". Then you hear the "very lonely...isolated sniffling" of a BFF of the decease, during the Eulogy. Young "Americans"...this is your time...but trust me... if this continue, you will not have the luxury of growing Old with your School classmates. We're still talking about Homosexuality.

PEOPLE...WAKE UP...LOOK AROUND YOU!!! Ask yourself these questions.

Are you openly supporting this behavior in your family? Have you not confronted someone in your family to let them know what the "*Leviticus 20:13* scriptures says about this lifestyle...and you know better? The nationwide legalization and publication of Homosexuality is doing all this to you and your love ones.

Because of this Leviticus scriptures is from the Book of OT "Law", the "Law enforcement of cities" has come under attack for committing deaths in America. I am saying, this Scripture(*Leviticus 20:13*) coming from OT Law is manipulating the atmosphere, creating incidence, involving Law enforcement resulting in questionable deaths. This is mostly targeting African-Americans. Its time for African-Americans to start asking this question to themselves without blaming it all on Race: "Why is this happening to us?"

Yes, the Police officer may be racist, but the real answer lies with the Almighty. I concluded that the Negro in slavery was like the Israelite in slavery. Neither of these two sets of slaves were going to be freed until they believe God was the only one could do this. And when they did believe, they were both freed... Israelite and Negro Slaves.

Both Races freedom was granted to uphold God's words, whether anyone else did or not. Because, the African-Americans has not done that as a whole: evil is coming upon them. God's has even introduce the word "*Karma*" in social gathering to help...*what you do will come back to you.* And has instructed me to leave this Scripture to the African Americans, *Revelation 2:4 Nevertheless, I have somewhat against thee, because thou hast left thy first love.*

The Black people has left their first love with God. And has left their first love of the Republican Party the tool God use to bring their Freedom. When they did this, they deny the name of a great OT patriot God use in executing their freedom: Abraham... surname, Lincoln the President. The Second Greatest name in Bible History. Because...Bible Abraham, initiated the coming messiah.

The Democrat party that African-American support, is the Party that enslaved them and now supporting the evil of Homosexuality in the nation..

This evil coming upon Black America has to do with the evil of racism down in their heart. African-Americans doesn't understand, in many cases, it takes as much racism to accuse racism...as the accuser of Racism. Black people are just as racist as the people they call racist. When I was growing up I heard, *"It take one to know one"*. Throughout history, the only credible racism, is when a member of the same race that is accuse of racism, agreed with the accuser. In other words, when a White man agreed with A Black man that he is being discriminated upon by the white man...that is a credible racial claim. If you study history. this is the only time major action has been enforce that made a change.

Another way to put this. When Obama was elected President in 2008. If a Black person voted for him...solely...because he was Black, you where no better than the White man that voted against him...solely...because he was Black. The only real credible vote of Obama in his elections, are the White people that voted for him. I know Black Republicans, that voted for him, just...because...he was Black. And I know loyal White Democrats(many)of Obama's own party, that voted against him; just...because...he was Black.

166

This is type of racial hatred in both Black and White people generates the evil of Homosexuality. Their is as many Black homosexual as there are white; based on population. You are not going to tell me, that the curse of mass homosexuality in our nation, has nothing to do with mass racial hatred of the Black and White race.

In light of this information, we hope that it is clear; although there are no laws in our nation today to punish the Homosexual life style; God still administer punishments in modern times equivalent to OT Law. His punishment is a demonstration, to let one know, that OT Law and NT Scriptures against homosexual is still enforced today. In doing this, he fulfills the scripture: *Heaven and earth shall pass away: but my words shall not pass away(Luke 21:33).*

In making the Homosexual choice, it has the potential of Genocide to a nation that endorses such a behavior.

Genocide will come in the form of natural disasters like floods and earthquakes. But right now, mass murder seems to be the punishment; which is actually following the guide lines of the OT Law(*Leviticus 20:13).*

The New Testaments is consistent with the Old Testaments on Same Sex Relationships. However, the difference between OT Law and NT Scriptures is, that NT scriptures offers hope through Jesus Christ. But because of the legalization of Same Sex Marriage in our nation; no one is seeking this "HOPE". That is why this book was authorize to be written.

For years, in modern times, man was looking for the cause and a cure for Homosexuality. But now that the Supreme Court has legalized Same Sex Marriage and the media is pushing the public acceptance of this ungodly behavior, no one is concern about the cure.

This book has revealed, that the first act of "Homosexuality-incest" was discovered in Noah's family after the flood. Which down through the ages, this behavior is caused by a darkness born out of extreme hate. It is believed, in America, that this hate is generated on a mass scale resulting from the Civil War over freeing the Negro slaves.

We have associated Homosexuality with Slavery throughout this book for good reason. The moment man listen and obeyed the Devil he would be a slave to sin from that point on. That is why two groups of people had to endure slavery.

Regardless, of the origin of Homosexuality and its vileness; there is a cure.

The cure on a personal level with the right mind set is found in the NT through Baptism *in the name of Jesus Christ(Acts 2:38)*. Because Same Sex Relationships has been legalized nation wide, a mass cure is needed for the nation now. This mass cure can come in a mass Baptism from God, in the form of a Flood. Or... this mass cure can come through the Government in the form of a Political Party...*Theocratic*; revamping the Atmosphere.

It was the Government that poked their head where it didn't belong. Just to find out, that our present form of Government, is not equipped to handle this kind of issue.

This book, hopefully has explained, how this evil is generated through our Government title name of Democracy: *Demon-create*. We have proven, that Homosexuality is a religious issue; therefore, an antidote, in the form of a religious political party is recommended.

This book concluded, that the only party that can do this, is "*Theocratic*": formulated from two Greek words *Theo* and *kratos*... with the definition..."*God Power*". By the original Bible coming from Greek scrolls; this gives the name *Theocratic*...a Greek derivative base; a Great power in changing the Atmosphere. In other words, the original Greek words of the Bible in *"Theocratic"* are Powerful enough to change the atmosphere back to Garden of Eden purity...*will be done on earth as it is in Heaven.*

But before we get to fixing the atmosphere with the *Theocratic party;* the Supreme Court verdict of declaring DOMA unconstitutional must be overturn.

The only fair solution on an issue such as this, that strikes at the very essence of civilization and mankind; must be settle through the Democratic process. That is; Government of the people, by the people, and for the people. ___A national vote must be held on this issue including every voting age American.___

Legalizing this behavior is bringing God's wrath upon this nation in the form of mass murders; but there is another fear worst than that

It is my belief, that if the Government doesn't put some kind of "Gag order" of publicizing Homosexuality; hate groups will rise up worse than the KKK against the freed Negro in the 19th century.

The KKK said that their flaming burning Cross supported Jesus Christ's teaching. But when the KKK began lynching and killing innocent people, that flaming Cross became a desecration to the teaching of Jesus Christ. Just goes to show how Bigotry blinds you.

They committed murder on innocent people and had "No scripture" to back them up. What do you think is going to happen when a group such as this rise up against Homosexuality? They have both OT Law and NT Scripture to support their killing. Listen to what *John 16:2* says in the "Bible Red letter" words of Jesus...*the time cometh that whosoever killeth you will think that he doeth God's service.* Even the scriptures let you know, that whatever happens to you, is your own fault for wanting to publicize your sexual orientation...*their blood should be upon their own head(Leviticus 20:13"*. And to add to this; I have seem more Bible scripture fulfilled under the Obama Presidency than I have seem my entire life.

Of course, the argument that will come from some Ministers who are "Gay sympathizer" is that, we are not under OT Law... that is true. But "circumcision", which was first done as a Religious ritual for a covenant between God and Patriot Abraham, is under OT Law. The reason I introduce the term "circumcision", is what the Apostle Paul of NT scriptures had to say on this subject.

Paul, one of the New Testament advocate for Jesus Christ said; that if *you are circumcised you are dector*(indebted*) to do the whole Law.(Galatian 5:3)* The whole Law includes the *Leviticus 20:13* scripture we have quoted throughout this message. That doesn't just mean Church Goers, it mean if "circumcision" is performed on you...the Gay; you're included. Also, circumcision is a practice perform on almost every male child born in the world of today. How many Gay men you think are circumcised? How many Lesbian's daddy are circumcised? So...that Scriptures applies to both the circumcised Gay and any "Gay hate group". That scripture permits a "Gay hate group" to bring harm to you and that same scripture make you their victim. Meaning that, such Anti-Gay groups can carry out violence with the Greatest judgment and support on earth..."The Holy Bible". We are already seeing the affects of this right now. So whatever harm that is brought upon the Gays, are blamed on President Obama and the five-four Supreme Court ruling.

Keep in mind; it doesn't matter, that in Hospitals of today, circumcision at birth is done for disease or infection purposes; it was instituted thousands of years ago for Religious reasons(*Genesis 17:1-27*). There are no statue of limitation on God's word.

Of course, another argument is...circumcision of the Heart(*Romans 2:29)*. There is a distinct difference of internal circumcision of the heart and external circumcision of the penis. Paul was pretty clear on which one he was referring, when he used the word "Law" in the above scripture.

As you can see, from the Bible history on a common every day practice like physical circumcision on male children, there are too many ways that the publicity of Homosexuality is not good. That is why, in the outset of this message, we used a Genesis Scripture, that gave the God ordained companion for man....women.

We hope that this book has proven; that the man and woman couple is the only companionship for love, marriage and sex God approves as being in his image. We also hope, that regardless of your intellect; if you are in a Same Sex Relationship; which stops procreation, this behavior ranks lower than the animals. Why? Because animals, instinctively know, how to continue their species through procreation. That is why the word *"Abomination"* is the proper term for Same Sex couples. Man not only suppose to be a pro-creator like the animals; but a Co-creator with God that separate him from the animals.

We hoped that understanding the first act of Homosexuality in Noah's family, gave new insight as to why and when slavery was ordained. Many people never understood the institute of slavery and its purpose. It was recommended by man(of God) and enforced by God. But wasn't intended to be an earthly eternal punishment. It was done for our learning. To let us know, we can be cursed as a group, as well as an individual. This also gave the understanding, of why there were a Bible race of people that were slaves and American race of people that were slaves as well. How both groups of slaves has shaped world History throughout time. But most importantly, how the abolishing of slavery in America has contributed to the out of control problem of Homosexuality of today.

The hate of the Black and White races generated from the Civil War cursed some families descendants of modern times as Homosexuals. With that, we hope that we have proven unequivocally, that Homosexuality is a curse. Meaning, not to be paraded as a good thing in society.

I hoped that this book has made it clear, that people's outraged of this behavior is not *discrimination;* but an *Abomination.* Meaning that, people's *disgust* and *hatred* of this lifestyle is natural and expected; supported by OT law and NT scriptures.

This book points out in many differ ways, how this is a personal and private matter because of its violation of God's sacred word in both OT Law and NT Scripture. It is part of the God plan of "choice"; established in the Garden of Eden from Adam and Eve's first commandment. Modern man has interpret this "choice" as "free will".

It is the kind of choice, that one is to be a shame of. The word "Abomination" suppose to have made that part of this behavior clear. This is why one suppose to keep it in the privacy of their own home between you and God. But when you publicize this as Good, and it is described as an evil, according to the Bible...is when you incur God's wrath upon us as a nation.

This is the way a conversation suppose to go between a true Heterosexual that has suspicions of a Homosexual: **Heterosexual**: "Are you Gay"? **Homosexual**: "My sexual orientation is none of your business". "Furthermore, what I do in the privacy of my own home is my business". "I am not bothering you". That response is true if you are "not" making a public confession of your sexual orientation. It is not the business of the *Public* "who you do" and "what you do" in the privacy of your home and bedroom.

This desire of wanting to publicized your "Same Sex" orientation....let me just put it bluntly...."Is A Death Sentence". This life choice violates too many Religions. Don't let Obama and the Supreme Court get you kill or shorten your life. YES... people will be punish for bringing harm to you. But the damage will already be done when this happen. Do you want to be "Dead Wrong" as well?

This book has illustrated, that we are a chosen people of God. This land was ordained from its very discovery by Christopher Columbus for a religious purpose. When God gave us this land and the Bible, as the tool to guide us; if the Bible says an act is wrong...then its wrong.

It is hoped that this book is able to convince the reader, that when we obey God's word and do the right things, we are blessed both individually as a person and collectively as a nation.

We hope that this book has given new insight as to how words and names at the pinnacle of power, can have good and adverse affect in the atmosphere; causing a domino affect to the inhabitants of the land. We hope that you, the reader, can see how in the last eight years, the Presidents(Obama) name has contributed greatly to the Homosexual issue with it being out control in America.

We hope that, one can see, that Same Sex couples has no business raising children. Understanding, that *whether you are Gay or Straight it require a male and female to birth you in the world.* By allowing Same Sex Couples to raise children, this take away the choice of a child to be Gay or Straight. From the very beginning with the first couple; Adam and Eve, choice has always been God's rule. Meaning that, this is the God ordain pattern all children are govern by: dad and mom...male and female. Hoping that one understands, that once you choose the Homosexual lifestyle; you void your right to raise children.

It is hoped, that it is clear to the powers to be, that no modern day law of man is going to cancel out a three thousand year old; OT Law enforced by Moses against Same Sex Relationship. And equally, no modern day law of man, is going to cancel out any two thousand year NT Scriptures against Same Sex Relationship...

preached by Paul and the other Apostles; whom all, were ordained by Jesus Christ. God backs up his chosen, and their messages; whether four thousand years ago; or...today. There are no "statue of limitation" placed on OT Law and NT Scripture in the eyes of God.

It is hoped, that from this book, the Gay community and its supporters, understand, that no law by the Government is going to protect you from the consequences resulting from you publicizing your Sexual orientation. That is what God's word says.

Because..the non-acceptance of Same Sex Relationship by Religious believers, is not *discrimination;* it is an *Abomination. Leviticus 18:22 and 20:13.* That is God's word.

As the nation first Black President winds down his final year in office we are completing the first and most important mission of America. Ending the curse of Servitude through the Obama Presidency. But in completing the task of ending the servitude curse as the "Nation mission"; we have legalized the cause.... Homosexuality.

The question I end with: is this God's Plan?

Immediately, following that question I decided to take a break. So I decided to scan my computer to see what was happening in the world. The first thing I saw was this news bulletin **"50 dead in gay nightclub shooting, worst in US history".** I said, "Oh My God" that is too much of a coincidence with me wrapping up the first draft of this book. I took this as God's confirmation that he ordain me to write this book. This is the interpretation of that Headline to me.

The "50" in that headline represent the United States of America. Biblical, fifty(50) is the number Bible Abraham started with; in his plead to the Angels to spare Sodom and Gomorrah.

(*Genesis 18:24-33*). The timing of this News event left me with this messages from God. First; this was the end of my book. Secondly, "fifty dead" as the beginning of the end, of publicizing Same Sex Relationships in America".

I hope that this book has given you something to think about. Hoping that you can understand, that Homosexuality affects more than just the institute of marriage ordain by God between a man and woman...it affects the future of our existence and favor with God.

That was suppose to be my last sentence in this Book. But last night(9/8/2016) I had this dream that I could fly. And all of sudden, other people begin to take flyth as well. Before daybreak, it was revealed....that the dream was about the *"Second coming of Christ"*... modern day Christians refer as the "Rapture". So I got up and begin to proofread and edit this Book. Reading over a sentence while editing this work, I voice requested my "Cell phone" with this command: *"Give me all scriptures on female Homosexuality"*. To my surprise, these art the scriptures that came up.

*Luke 17:34-36: I tell you, in that night there shall be **two men in one bed**; the one shall be taken, and the other shall be left. (35)**Two women shall be grinding together**; the one shall be taken, and the other left.(36) Two men shall be in the field; the one shall be taken, and the other left.* These three scriptures were in "Red letters", meaning that, Jesus spoke them.

I have read the Bible "straight through three times" in my life and never remember those scriptures. However, I did remember the reference scriptures to these *Luke 17* scriptures...found in *Matthew 24:40-41 Then shall two be in the field, the one shall be taken, and the other left. Two women shall be grinding at the mill; the one shall be taken and the other left.*

The revelation of those scriptures help me finally understand over the years; what the Book of *Job 33:15-16* meant in those Scriptures: *In a dream, in a vision of the night, when deep sleep falleth* *upon men, in slumberings upon the bed; Then he openeth the ears of men, and sealeth their instruction,...*The dream I had...was about the *"Second Coming of Christ"* and God sealed my instruction for the day that guided me when daybreak came to those scriptures. The *Luke 17th* chapter ends, with the *"second coming of Christ"*.

The big question in the *Luke 17* scriptures above: is Jesus speaking about Same Sex couples? After all, He said *"two men in one bed"*. The Gospel of *Matthew* got in on the same sermon Jesus was teaching. But the *Matthew 24* Chapters didn't mention the *"two men in one bed"*. The *Matthew 24:41* scripture with *the two women grinding together* substituted the phrase *"at the mill"* for the word *"together"*. Both of these chapters(*Luke 17th and Matthew 24th)*) are referring to the *"second coming of Christ"*.

In our explanation, let's not loose the point of these scriptures. The point of these scriptures, are to let you know, the *"second coming of Christ"* can come when least expected...catching you off guard, unprepared, and doing something out of God's Will.

Nevertheless, the *Luke 17:34* scriptures says, *"Two men together in one bed"* It doesn't specify what was going on between the men. In the OT, the *Leviticus 20:13* is very specific. *If man also lieth with mankind as he lieth with a woman, both of them have committed an abomination: they shall surely be put to death: their blood shall be upon them.*

And then the *Luke 17:35* says, the *"two women grinding together"*... the *"**WAY**"* that scripture is written, is without a doubt, referring to a Lesbian couple having sex. The book of *Job 31:9-10* support that. Read what the scripture says; Job is speaking: *If mine heart have been deceived by a woman, or if I have laid wait at my neighbour's door; Then let my wife **grind** unto another, and let others bow down upon her.* By reading that scripture, with the use of the word *"grind"*, it is definite making reference to sexual intercourse. The*"bow down upon her"* is part of the sexual process in that scripture as well. *Hebrew 13:4* explains that phrase this way: *Marriaage is honourable in all,and the bed undefiled: but whoremongers and adulterers God will judge.*

176

The first part of that scriptures refers to traditional marriage of man and woman: meaning, anything goes in love making between a husband and wife. The last part of that scripture, includes the Homosexual...*whoremongers and adulterers God will judge.*

Nevertheless, the question still remain: why did *Matthew* hear *grinding at the mill* and *Luke* heard *grinding together?* Whether its *two men in one bed* or *two women having sex,* **it still doesn't say that Jesus condoms Homosexuality.** However, it does indicate, that Jesus mention Homosexuality indirectly. But the *Leviticus 20:13 OT* Scriptures by Moses, and the NT Scriptures by Apostles, describes sex between the same gender...clearly; and a violation of God's will with severe consequences.

I will "NOT" try to twist these two *Luke 17* scriptures to mean anything other than Gay couples...because of the "WAY" the scriptures are written. Also, believe it or not, I once search the Bible to find scriptures to support Homosexuality. I...like a lot of people, felt that same sex relationships are your personal and private business. But when it begin to be publicized through legalization, something felt wrong about that. When God let me know, that publicizing this Homosexual behavior was wrong, this book was initiated.

Nevertheless, referring to the two *Luke 17* scriptures above: does this mean that some Homosexuals are going to be spared? Those scriptures could be "An Eleven Hour Reprieve" in each case of one partner of a Same Sex relationship. There are scriptures that support the "eleven hour reprieve" idea, but no scriptures that suggest exemption from the *"Same Sex Sin Penalty"* all together.

At the exact moment of the *"second coming of Christ,* one of the partners could become convince that Same Sex Relationship is wrong while performing(*"grinding"*). This is the Mercy of the Christ Jesus that I have been taught.

Here are scriptures that support "The Eleven Hour Reprieve" idea. The *Matthew 20:1-12* ...referring to the man that hired workers that worked all day receiving the same pay as the man that work only one hour before the work day ended. This is a parable by Jesus to his disciples...meaning; whether you repented forty years ago and been following Christ ever since, or repented in the last second-moment; the *"reward for Salvation of both times are the same"*.

Let's not forget the "thieve", that was hanging next to Jesus on the cross.(*Luke 23:43*) The thieve hanging on the cross dying; a breath or two away from death, and Jesus tells him, you are going to Heaven with me today(*"this day you will be with me in Paradise"*). You can't get much closer than that, of an "eleven hour reprieve".

In the *Luke* Scripture, about the *two men in one bed*; Jesus start that scripture with "*I tell You*"...he is talking to people like "ME" ...the author of this Book. That phrase "*I tell You*" is the same as me saying "You Are Not Going to Believe This" or "Believe It or Not" *there will be two men in one bed one taken and the other left"*.

The vagueness of the *two men in one bed* scripture, and the substitute wording between the *"Matthew and Luke* scriptures *of the two women grinding together(at the mill)* is to let the Homosexual know, there is "Hope" for them. Simply, because of the "Way" it is written. And that Jesus, is going to have the last say...the same as he did for the women that was brought to him caught in the very act of adultery(*John 8:3-11*). The above mention *Hebrew 13:4* scriptures support the fact that Jesus will have the last words when it says: *"whoremongers and adulterers God will Judge."*

Just so that we are clear on this; there will not be any "eleventh hour reprieve" for anyone whom has read this book or the Preface. Those scripture does not in any way "negate" any information in this book. The "eleventh Hour reprieve", is for an elect child of God whom have gotten caught up in this behavior because the President and Supreme court legalized it, and it hit them at the last moment that Same Sex relation is wrong. This.... "eleventh hour reprieve" we are referring to, is a Homosexual that has ask for forgiveness and is trying "**DESPERATELY**" to get out of a Same Sex relationship.

After presenting all these speculations of what the *Luke 17:34 & 35* scriptures were making reference too; God gave me the final Revelation. These scriptures was given at the end of this book to support the major theme of this message. And that is, why you *should not be publicizing your Homosexuality....why it is a private matter that you should keep it to yourself.* If you keep this behavior between you and God, then God will be a merciful and a fair judge. By keeping it to yourself, you understand the shame of this behavior.

He will take in consideration, how you accepted the responsibility of this choice as your own. How you did not force your family, and this nation to indulge your life choice; of which, the Bible is totally against. He will take in consideration, how you did not practice this behavior in front of children....confusing them. This means to me, that there are some that cannot help themselves with their Homosexuality...the definition of a curse. Meaning, this behavior was dumped on you, as we mention in this message earlier by an ancestor.

On the other hand, when you publicized your Homosexuality, you back God in a corner. God "HAS TO" support Moses OT Leviticus Law and the Apostles NT scriptures on this issues. I stated above; God will back up his anointed and chosen. The Apostle Peter in *II Peter 1:20* stated...*no prophecy of the scripture is of any private interpretation.*

When the Religious people are quoting scriptures, with clarity of meaning to you on your Homosexual life choice, you are bound by those scriptures. And when you keep a life choice like Homosexuality to yourself, no one is going to be isolating and quoting scriptures directly to you. Once the Publicity of Same Sex Marriage stop; the finger pointing of Scriptures will stop as well. *Interpretation of scriptures may not be private,* but what you do can be.

When you publicize your Homosexuality; you make a mockery of God's word and his servants. The *Luke 17:34&35* scriptures are mostly, referring to those whom have kept their sexual orientation to themselves. This is what Jesus was referring to when he use the phrase: *I tell you.*

And with that, we have discuss throughout this book ways to correct the Homosexual problem in America. We mention a Nation wide vote...a New Political Party and how God has responded to sin in the pass through earthquakes and floods. But there is another plan..the final plan..."*The Second Coming Of Christ*". I can't help from wondering, in light of this new information in the *Luke 17th* chapter and the *Matthew 24th* chapter....is God telling me, its too late for these other plans discussed throughout this message?

After the five-four ruling in 2015; declaring DOMA unconstitutional, I ask God the same question Abraham, the Bible patriot, ask the Angels before he started to plead for Sodom and Gomorrah. The question Abraham ask was..."*Will thou also destroy the righteous with the wicked?(Genesis 18:23)* The answer I received was.

The last and final plan to solve the Homosexual problem is to take the righteous out through the *"second coming"*: some call the Rapture. That is what my dream was about, that led me to the above two scriptures in *St. Luke* and *St. Matthew*.

I like to close this book with this. In the chapter that referred to my "Early Experience and Inspiration for this book" I compared my Birth name *Luby* with similarities of the NT Gospel writer St. *Luke*. I did this because *St. Luke* was the name given to the Church my family built one hundred ten years ago. Now I realize why I was led to do that. Because, the most pertinent New Testament information on whether Jesus spoke directly or indirectly on Homosexuals was in the Gospel of *St. Luke*. Also *Luke*, the Gospel writer was a physician. In likeness, I was name after the physician that delivered me at birth. I hope that this book has brought "Healing" to someone. It is Finish!!!

About the Book Cover

When it came to the Book cover, God let me know, to remind us how it all started. We have included all the participants. We have Adam, Eve, The tree of knowledge, the forbidden fruit and the Serpent. This was not the original appearance of the serpents...a snake: this is what his action of seducing Eve to bite the forbidden fruit turned him to.

The cover reminds us, that God gave the first couple a commandment. *"Don't eat of the tree of knowledge of Good and Evil."* By Eve gazing at the forbidden fruit, another voice came in her mind. With smooth talk and partial trues, the first commandment was broken. The serpent gave Eve a very compelling and convincing logic on why she should eat the forbidden fruit. Only hearing one side of the story from God her father, and not being informed of another side...she gave in to the Serpent.

As I watch T.V. Series and movies on support of Homosexuality; they gives very compelling and I must say, "heart warming" stories as well. The T.V. Lawyers present their cases with such convincing facts...you just have to say WOW.

You know if Lawyers in real life can get a person off a murder charge with "several" eyewitnesses; a T.V. Producer can write a script for a T.V. Lawyer with a convincing plea for the Homosexual. Producing arguments like: "how this is right to allow Same Sex Marriage"....how a person should follow the dictation of their mind rather than body" etc. Then the T.V. scenes with the father having a change of heart defending his Gay Son or Daughter is very touching. *This all just goes to show one thing; after thousands of years...the Devil "Has Not lost his touch".*

The world is still paying for what he done to Eve in the Garden of Eden. You see Eve...bless her little heart, only had one command and statement to go on. But you the reader, have a volume with 66 books(Holy Bible) within it, and millions of books written to explain those 66 books of the "Holy Bible". There will not be any excuses for you. You have read about the punishment, Adam and Eve receive with just the one commandment...and a very short commandment at that. What do you thinks its going to be like for you with all this information?

The world has paid several thousand years and..even erase the first world and started over(Noah's Flood) for Eve being seduce by the Devil. And the five-four ruling of our Supreme court is causing a Nation to pay for another sin Satan has convince man of. That is the sin to end procreation through Same Sex Marriage. Sending a message throughout the Atmosphere of Genocide. Ending the continuity of our species.

Proverbs 14:12 There is a way which seemeth right unto a man, but the end thereof are the ways of death. Homosexuality never seem right to me.

Appendix A

References:

The Holy Bible, King James Version

Encyclopedia Britannica

The Computer: Wikipedia, the free Encyclopedia

The Light and Glory by Peter Marshall and David Manuel

His Hallowed Name Revealed Again, by Keith E. Johnson

Super Being, by Randolph Price

You can Heal your life, by Louis L. Hay

Your Maximum Mind, by Hervert Benson, M.C.

Television Series "Arrow"

Television Series "Supernatural"

The Movie "Superman vs Batman"

Television series "Smallville"